Basic Numeracy
and Statistics

Second Edition

Basic Numeracy and Statistics

Selected chapters from

Foundation Maths
Fifth Edition
Anthony Croft and Robert Davison

Harlow, England • London • New York • Boston • San Francisco • Toronto • Sydney • Auckland • Singapore • Hong Kong
Tokyo • Seoul • Taipei • New Delhi • Cape Town • Sao Paulo • Mexico City • Madrid • Amsterdam • Munich • Paris • Milan

Pearson Education Limited
Edinburgh Gate
Harlow
Essex CM20 2JE

And associated companies throughout the world

Visit us on the World Wide Web at:
www.pearson.com/uk

First published 2014
This edition © Pearson Education Limited 2015

Selected chapters from:

Foundation Maths
Fifth Edition
Anthony Croft and Robert Davison
978-0-273-72940-2
© Pearson Education Limited 1995, 2010

ISBN 978-1-78434-565-5

Printed and bound in Great Britain by Ashford Colour Press, Gosport, Hampshire.

Contents

The following is taken from
Foundation Maths Fifth Edition
Anthony Croft and Robert Davison

Mathematical symbols

$+$	plus
$-$	minus
$\pm$	plus or minus
$\times$	multiply by
$\cdot$	multiply by
$\div$	divide by
$=$	is equal to
$\equiv$	is identically equal to
$\approx$	is approximately equal to
$\neq$	is not equal to
$>$	is greater than
$\geqslant$	is greater than or equal to
$<$	is less than
$\leqslant$	is less than or equal to
$\in$	is a member of set
$\mathcal{E}$	universal set
$\cap$	intersection
$\cup$	union
$\emptyset$	empty set
$\bar{A}$	complement of set A
$\subseteq$	subset
$\mathbb{R}$	all real numbers
$\mathbb{R}^+$	all numbers greater than 0
$\mathbb{R}^-$	all numbers less than 0
$\mathbb{Z}$	all integers
$\mathbb{N}$	all positive integers

$\mathbb{Q}$ rational numbers

Π irrational numbers

$\therefore$ therefore

∞ infinity

e the base of natural logarithms (2.718 ...)

ln   natural logarithm

log   logarithm to base 10

$\sum$ sum of terms

$\int$ integral

$\frac{dy}{dx}$ derivative of y with respect to x

π 'pi' ≈ 3.14159

$\neg$ negation (not)

$\wedge$ conjunction (and)

$\vee$ disjunction (or)

$\rightarrow$ implication

Arithmetic of whole numbers

1

03

Objectives: This chapter:

- explains the rules for adding, subtracting, multiplying and dividing positive and negative numbers
- explains what is meant by an integer
- explains what is meant by a prime number
- explains what is meant by a factor
- explains how to prime factorise an integer
- explains the terms 'highest common factor' and 'lowest common multiple'

1.1 Addition, subtraction, multiplication and division

Arithmetic is the study of numbers and their manipulation. A clear and firm understanding of the rules of arithmetic is essential for tackling everyday calculations. Arithmetic also serves as a springboard for tackling more abstract mathematics such as algebra and calculus.

The calculations in this chapter will involve mainly whole numbers, or **integers** as they are often called. The **positive integers** are the numbers

$$1, 2, 3, 4, 5 \ldots$$

and the **negative integers** are the numbers

$$\ldots -5, -4, -3, -2, -1$$

The dots (...) indicate that this sequence of numbers continues indefinitely. The number 0 is also an integer but is neither positive nor negative.

To find the **sum** of two or more numbers, the numbers are added together. To find the **difference** of two numbers, the second is subtracted from the first. The **product** of two numbers is found by multiplying the numbers together. Finally, the **quotient** of two numbers is found by dividing the first number by the second.

WORKED EXAMPLE

1.1   (a) Find the sum of 3, 6 and 4.

(b) Find the difference of 6 and 4.

(c) Find the product of 7 and 2.

(d) Find the quotient of 20 and 4.

Solution   (a) The sum of 3, 6 and 4 is

$$3 + 6 + 4 = 13$$

(b) The difference of 6 and 4 is

$$6 - 4 = 2$$

(c) The product of 7 and 2 is

$$7 \times 2 = 14$$

(d) The quotient of 20 and 4 is $\frac{20}{4}$, that is 5.

When writing products we sometimes replace the sign $\times$ by '·' or even omit it completely. For example, $3 \times 6 \times 9$ could be written as $3 \cdot 6 \cdot 9$ or $(3)(6)(9)$.

On occasions it is necessary to perform calculations involving negative numbers. To understand how these are added and subtracted consider Figure 1.1, which shows a number line.

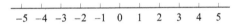

Figure 1.1
The number line

Any number can be represented by a point on the line. Positive numbers are on the right-hand side of the line and negative numbers are on the left. From any given point on the line, we can add a positive number by moving that number of places to the right. For example, to find the sum $5 + 3$, start at the point 5 and move 3 places to the right, to arrive at 8. This is shown in Figure 1.2.

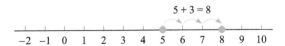

Figure 1.2
To add a positive number, move that number of places to the right

To subtract a positive number, we move that number of places to the left. For example, to find the difference $5 - 7$, start at the point 5 and move 7 places to the left to arrive at -2. Thus $5 - 7 = -2$. This is shown in Figure 1.3. The result of finding $-3 - 4$ is also shown to be -7.

Figure 1.3

To subtract a positive number, move that number of places to the left

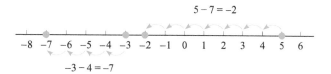

To add or subtract a negative number, the motions just described are reversed. So, to add a negative number, we move to the left. To subtract a negative number we move to the right. The result of finding $2 + (-3)$ is shown in Figure 1.4.

Figure 1.4

Adding a negative number involves moving to the left

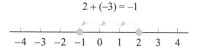

We see that $2 + (-3) = -1$. Note that this is the same as the result of finding $2 - 3$, so that adding a negative number is equivalent to subtracting a positive number.

Figure 1.5

Subtracting a negative number involves moving to the right

The result of finding $5 - (-3)$ is shown in Figure 1.5.

We see that $5 - (-3) = 8$. This is the same as the result of finding $5 + 3$, so subtracting a negative number is equivalent to adding a positive number.

Key point

Adding a negative number is equivalent to subtracting a positive number.
Subtracting a negative number is equivalent to adding a positive number.

WORKED EXAMPLE

1.2   Evaluate (a) $8 + (-4)$, (b) $-15 + (-3)$, (c) $-15 - (-4)$.

Solution   (a) $8 + (-4)$ is equivalent to $8 - 4$, that is 4.

(b) Because adding a negative number is equivalent to subtracting a positive number we find $-15 + (-3)$ is equivalent to $-15 - 3$, that is -18.

(c) $-15 - (-4)$ is equivalent to $-15 + 4$, that is -11.

When we need to multiply or divide negative numbers, care must be taken with the **sign** of the answer; that is, whether the result is positive or negative. The following rules apply for determining the sign of the answer when multiplying or dividing positive and negative numbers.

Key point

(positive) $\times$ (positive) $=$ positive   and

(positive) $\times$ (negative) $=$ negative

(negative) $\times$ (positive) $=$ negative

(negative) $\times$ (negative) $=$ positive

$$\frac{\text{positive}}{\text{positive}} = \text{positive}$$

$$\frac{\text{positive}}{\text{negative}} = \text{negative}$$

$$\frac{\text{negative}}{\text{positive}} = \text{negative}$$

$$\frac{\text{negative}}{\text{negative}} = \text{positive}$$

WORKED EXAMPLE

1.3   Evaluate

(a) $3 \times (-2)$ (b) $(-1) \times 7$ (c) $(-2) \times (-4)$ (d) $\dfrac{12}{(-4)}$ (e) $\dfrac{-8}{4}$ (f) $\dfrac{-6}{-2}$

Solution   (a) We have a positive number, 3, multiplied by a negative number, -2, and so the result will be negative:

$$3 \times (-2) = -6$$

(b) $(-1) \times 7 = -7$

(c) Here we have two negative numbers being multiplied and so the result will be positive:

$$(-2) \times (-4) = 8$$

(d) A positive number, 12, divided by a negative number, -4, gives a negative result:

$$\frac{12}{-4} = -3$$

(e) A negative number, -8, divided by a positive number, 4, gives a negative result:

$$\frac{-8}{4} = -2$$

(f) A negative number, -6, divided by a negative number, -2, gives a positive result:

$$\frac{-6}{-2} = 3$$

Self-assessment questions 1.1

1. Explain what is meant by an integer, a positive integer and a negative integer.

2. Explain the terms sum, difference, product and quotient.

3. State the sign of the result obtained after performing the following calculations:
    (a) $(-5) \times (-3)$ (b) $(-4) \times 2$ (c) $\frac{7}{-2}$ (d) $\frac{-8}{-4}$.

Exercise 1.1

MyMathLab

1. Without using a calculator, evaluate each of the following:
    (a) $6 + (-3)$ (b) $6 - (-3)$
    (c) $16 + (-5)$ (d) $16 - (-5)$
    (e) $27 - (-3)$ (f) $27 - (-29)$
    (g) $-16 + 3$ (h) $-16 + (-3)$
    (i) $-16 - 3$ (j) $-16 - (-3)$
    (k) $-23 + 52$ (l) $-23 + (-52)$
    (m) $-23 - 52$ (n) $-23 - (-52)$

2. Without using a calculator, evaluate
    (a) $3 \times (-8)$ (b) $(-4) \times 8$ (c) $15 \times (-2)$
    (d) $(-2) \times (-8)$ (e) $14 \times (-3)$

3. Without using a calculator, evaluate
    (a) $\frac{15}{-3}$ (b) $\frac{21}{7}$ (c) $\frac{-21}{7}$ (d) $\frac{-21}{-7}$ (e) $\frac{21}{-7}$
    (f) $\frac{-12}{2}$ (g) $\frac{-12}{-2}$ (h) $\frac{12}{-2}$

4. Find the sum and product of (a) 3 and 6, (b) 10 and 7, (c) 2, 3 and 6.

5. Find the difference and quotient of (a) 18 and 9, (b) 20 and 5, (c) 100 and 20.

1.2 The BODMAS rule

When evaluating numerical expressions we need to know the order in which addition, subtraction, multiplication and division are carried out. As a simple example, consider evaluating $2 + 3 \times 4$. If the addition is carried out first we get $2 + 3 \times 4 = 5 \times 4 = 20$. If the multiplication is carried out first we get $2 + 3 \times 4 = 2 + 12 = 14$. Clearly the order of carrying out numerical operations is important. The BODMAS rule tells us the order in which we must carry out the operations of addition, subtraction, multiplication and division.

Key point	BODMAS stands for	
	Brackets ( )	First priority
	Of $\times$	Second priority
	Division $\div$	Second priority
	Multiplication $\times$	Second priority
	Addition $+$	Third priority
	Subtraction $-$	Third priority

This is the order of carrying out arithmetical operations, with bracketed expressions having highest priority and subtraction and addition having the lowest priority. Note that 'Of', 'Division' and 'Multiplication' have equal priority, as do 'Addition' and 'Subtraction'. 'Of' is used to show multiplication when dealing with fractions: for example, find $\frac{1}{2}$ of 6 means $\frac{1}{2} \times 6$.

If an expression contains only multiplication and division, we evaluate by working from left to right. Similarly, if an expression contains only addition and subtraction, we also evaluate by working from left to right.

WORKED EXAMPLES

1.4 Evaluate

(a) $2 + 3 \times 4$ (b) $(2 + 3) \times 4$

Solution   (a) Using the BODMAS rule we see that multiplication is carried out first. So

$$2 + 3 \times 4 = 2 + 12 = 14$$

(b) Using the BODMAS rule we see that the bracketed expression takes priority over all else. Hence

$$(2 + 3) \times 4 = 5 \times 4 = 20$$

1.5 Evaluate

(a) $4 - 2 \div 2$ (b) $1 - 3 + 2 \times 2$

Solution   (a) Division is carried out before subtraction, and so

$$4 - 2 \div 2 = 4 - \frac{2}{2} = 3$$

(b) Multiplication is carried out before subtraction or addition:

$$1 - 3 + 2 \times 2 = 1 - 3 + 4 = 2$$

1.6   Evaluate

(a) $(12 \div 4) \times 3$ (b) $12 \div (4 \times 3)$

Solution   Recall that bracketed expressions are evaluated first.

(a) $(12 \div 4) \times 3 = \left(\dfrac{12}{4} \right) \times 3 = 3 \times 3 = 9$

(b) $12 \div (4 \times 3) = 12 \div 12 = 1$

Example 1.6 shows the importance of the position of brackets in an expression.

Self-assessment questions 1.2

1. State the BODMAS rule used to evaluate expressions.

2. The position of brackets in an expression is unimportant. True or false?

Exercise 1.2

1. Evaluate the following expressions:
    (a) $6 - 2 \times 2$ (b) $(6 - 2) \times 2$
    (c) $6 \div 2 - 2$ (d) $(6 \div 2) - 2$
    (e) $6 - 2 + 3 \times 2$ (f) $6 - (2 + 3) \times 2$
    (g) $(6 - 2) + 3 \times 2$ (h) $\dfrac{16}{-2}$ (i) $\dfrac{-24}{-3}$
    (j) $(-6) \times (-2)$ (k) $(-2)(-3)(-4)$

2. Place brackets in the following expressions to make them correct:
    (a) $6 \times 12 - 3 + 1 = 55$
    (b) $6 \times 12 - 3 + 1 = 68$
    (c) $6 \times 12 - 3 + 1 = 60$
    (d) $5 \times 4 - 3 + 2 = 7$
    (e) $5 \times 4 - 3 + 2 = 15$
    (f) $5 \times 4 - 3 + 2 = -5$

1.3 Prime numbers and factorisation

A **prime number** is a positive integer, larger than 1, which cannot be expressed as the product of two smaller positive integers. To put it another way, a prime number is one that can be divided exactly only by 1 and itself.

For example, $6 = 2 \times 3$, so 6 can be expressed as a product of smaller numbers and hence 6 is not a prime number. However, 7 is prime. Examples of prime numbers are 2, 3, 5, 7, 11, 13, 17, 19, 23. Note that 2 is the only even prime.

Factorise means 'write as a product'. By writing 12 as 3×4 we have factorised 12. We say 3 is a **factor** of 12 and 4 is also a factor of 12. The way in which a number is factorised is not unique: for example, 12 may be expressed as 3×4 or 2×6. Note that 2 and 6 are also factors of 12.

When a number is written as a product of prime numbers we say the number has been **prime factorised**.

To prime factorise a number, consider the technique used in the following examples.

WORKED EXAMPLES

1.7   Prime factorise the following numbers:

(a) 12   (b) 42   (c) 40   (d) 70

Solution   (a) We begin with 2 and see whether this is a factor of 12. Clearly it is, so we write

$$12 = 2 \times 6$$

Now we consider 6. Again 2 is a factor so we write

$$12 = 2 \times 2 \times 3$$

All the factors are now prime, that is the prime factorisation of 12 is $2 \times 2 \times 3$.

(b) We begin with 2 and see whether this is a factor of 42. Clearly it is and so we can write

$$42 = 2 \times 21$$

Now we consider 21. Now 2 is not a factor of 21, so we examine the next prime, 3. Clearly 3 is a factor of 21 and so we can write

$$42 = 2 \times 3 \times 7$$

All the factors are now prime, and so the prime factorisation of 42 is $2 \times 3 \times 7$.

(c) Clearly 2 is a factor of 40,

$$40 = 2 \times 20$$

Clearly 2 is a factor of 20,

$$40 = 2 \times 2 \times 10$$

Again 2 is a factor of 10,

$$40 = 2 \times 2 \times 2 \times 5$$

All the factors are now prime. The prime factorisation of 40 is $2 \times 2 \times 2 \times 5$.

(d) Clearly 2 is a factor of 70,

$$70 = 2 \times 35$$

We consider 35: 2 is not a factor, 3 is not a factor, but 5 is:

$$70 = 2 \times 5 \times 7$$

All the factors are prime. The prime factorisation of 70 is $2 \times 5 \times 7$.

1.8   Prime factorise 2299.

Solution   We note that 2 is not a factor and so we try 3. Again 3 is not a factor and so we try 5. This process continues until we find the first prime factor. It is 11:

$$2299 = 11 \times 209$$

We now consider 209. The first prime factor is 11:

$$2299 = 11 \times 11 \times 19$$

All the factors are prime. The prime factorisation of 2299 is $11 \times 11 \times 19$.

Self-assessment questions 1.3

1. Explain what is meant by a prime number.

2. List the first 10 prime numbers.

3. Explain why all even numbers other than 2 cannot be prime.

Exercise 1.3

1. State which of the following numbers are prime numbers:
   (a) 13   (b) 1000   (c) 2   (c) 29   (d) $\frac{1}{2}$

2. Prime factorise the following numbers:
   (a) 26   (b) 100   (c) 27   (d) 71   (e) 64   (f) 87   (g) 437   (h) 899

3. Prime factorise the two numbers 30 and 42. List any prime factors which are common to both numbers.

1.4 Highest common factor and lowest common multiple

Highest common factor

Suppose we prime factorise 12. This gives $12 = 2 \times 2 \times 3$. From this prime factorisation we can deduce all the factors of 12:

2 is a factor of 12
3 is a factor of 12
$2 \times 2 = 4$ is a factor of 12
$2 \times 3 = 6$ is a factor of 12

Hence 12 has factors 2, 3, 4 and 6, in addition to the obvious factors of 1 and 12.

Similarly we could prime factorise 18 to obtain $18 = 2 \times 3 \times 3$. From this we can list the factors of 18:

2 is a factor of 18
3 is a factor of 18
$2 \times 3 = 6$ is a factor of 18
$3 \times 3 = 9$ is a factor of 18

The factors of 18 are 1, 2, 3, 6, 9 and 18. Some factors are common to both 12 and 18. These are 2, 3 and 6. These are **common factors** of 12 and 18. The highest common factor of 12 and 18 is 6.

The highest common factor of 12 and 18 can be obtained directly from their prime factorisation. We simply note all the primes common to both factorisations:

$$12 = 2 \times 2 \times 3 \qquad 18 = 2 \times 3 \times 3$$

Common to both is 2×3. Thus the highest common factor is $2 \times 3 = 6$. Thus 6 is the highest number that divides exactly into both 12 and 18.

Key point

Given two or more numbers the **highest common factor** (h.c.f.) is the largest (highest) number that is a factor of all the given numbers.
The highest common factor is also referred to as the **greatest common divisor** (g.c.d).

WORKED EXAMPLES

1.9   Find the h.c.f. of 12 and 27.

Solution   We prime factorise 12 and 27:

$$12 = 2 \times 2 \times 3 \qquad 27 = 3 \times 3 \times 3$$

Common to both is 3. Thus 3 is the h.c.f. of 12 and 27. This means that 3 is the highest number that divides both 12 and 27.

1.10   Find the h.c.f. of 28 and 210.

Solution   The numbers are prime factorised:

$$28 = 2 \times 2 \times 7$$
$$210 = 2 \times 3 \times 5 \times 7$$

The factors that are common are identified: a 2 is common to both and a 7 is common to both. Hence both numbers are divisible by $2 \times 7 = 14$. Since this number contains all the common factors it is the highest common factor.

1.11   Find the h.c.f. of 90 and 108.

Solution   The numbers are prime factorised:

$$90 = 2 \times 3 \times 3 \times 5$$
$$108 = 2 \times 2 \times 3 \times 3 \times 3$$

The common factors are 2, 3 and 3 and so the h.c.f. is $2 \times 3 \times 3$, that is 18. This is the highest number that divides both 90 and 108.

1.12   Find the h.c.f. of 12, 18 and 20.

Solution   Prime factorisation yields

$$12 = 2 \times 2 \times 3 \qquad 18 = 2 \times 3 \times 3 \qquad 20 = 2 \times 2 \times 5$$

There is only one factor common to all three numbers: it is 2. Hence 2 is the h.c.f. of 12, 18 and 20.

Lowest common multiple

Suppose we are given two or more numbers and wish to find numbers into which all the given numbers will divide. For example, given 4 and 6 we see that they both divide exactly into 12, 24, 36, 48, 60 and so on. The smallest number into which they both divide is 12. We say 12 is the **lowest common multiple** of 4 and 6.

Key point   The lowest common multiple (l.c.m.) of a set of numbers is the smallest (lowest) number into which all the given numbers will divide exactly.

WORKED EXAMPLE

1.13   Find the l.c.m. of 6 and 10.

Solution   We seek the smallest number into which both 6 and 10 will divide exactly. There are many numbers into which 6 and 10 will divide, for example 60,

120, 600, but we are seeking the smallest such number. By inspection, the smallest such number is 30. Thus the l.c.m. of 6 and 10 is 30.

A more systematic method of finding the l.c.m. involves the use of prime factorisation.

WORKED EXAMPLES

1.14   Find the l.c.m. of 15 and 20.

Solution   As a first step, the numbers are prime factorised:

$$15 = 3 \times 5 \qquad 20 = 2 \times 2 \times 5$$

Since 15 must divide into the l.c.m., then the l.c.m. must contain the factors of 15, that is 3×5. Similarly, as 20 must divide into the l.c.m., then the l.c.m. must also contain the factors of 20, that is $2 \times 2 \times 5$. The l.c.m. is the smallest number that contains both of these sets of factors. Note that the l.c.m. will contain only 2s, 3s and 5s as its prime factors. We now need to determine how many of these particular factors are needed.

To determine the l.c.m. we ask 'How many factors of 2 are required?', 'How many factors of 3 are required?', 'How many factors of 5 are required?'

The highest number of 2s occurs in the factorisation of 20. Hence the l.c.m. requires two factors of 2. Consider the number of 3s required. The highest number of 3s occurs in the factorisation of 15. Hence the l.c.m. requires one factor of 3. Consider the number of 5s required. The highest number of 5s is 1 and so the l.c.m. requires one factor of 5. Hence the l.c.m. is $2 \times 2 \times 3 \times 5 = 60$.

Hence 60 is the smallest number into which both 15 and 20 will divide exactly.

1.15   Find the l.c.m. of 20, 24 and 25.

Solution   The numbers are prime factorised:

$$20 = 2 \times 2 \times 5 \qquad 24 = 2 \times 2 \times 2 \times 3 \qquad 25 = 5 \times 5$$

By considering the prime factorisations of 20, 24 and 25 we see that the only primes involved are 2, 3 and 5. Hence the l.c.m. will contain only 2s, 3s and 5s.

Consider the number of 2s required. The highest number of 2s required is three from factorising 24. The highest number of 3s required is one, again from factorising 24. The highest number of 5s required is two, found from factorising 25. Hence the l.c.m. is given by

$$\text{l.c.m.} = 2 \times 2 \times 2 \times 3 \times 5 \times 5 = 600$$

Hence 600 is the smallest number into which 20, 24 and 25 will all divide exactly.

Self-assessment questions 1.4

1. Explain what is meant by the h.c.f. of a set of numbers.

2. Explain what is meant by the l.c.m. of a set of numbers.

Exercise 1.4

1. Calculate the h.c.f. of the following sets of numbers:
   (a) 12, 15, 21 (b) 16, 24, 40 (c) 28, 70, 120, 160 (d) 35, 38, 42 (e) 96, 120, 144

2. Calculate the l.c.m. of the following sets of numbers:
   (a) 5, 6, 8 (b) 20, 30 (c) 7, 9, 12 (d) 100, 150, 235 (e) 96, 120, 144

1. Evaluate
   (a) $6 \div 2 + 1$
   (b) $6 \div (2 + 1)$
   (c) $12 + 4 \div 4$
   (d) $(12 + 4) \div 4$
   (e) $3 \times 2 + 1$
   (f) $3 \times (2 + 1)$
   (g) $6 - 2 + 4 \div 2$
   (h) $(6 - 2 + 4) \div 2$
   (i) $6 - (2 + 4 \div 2)$
   (j) $6 - (2 + 4) \div 2$
   (k) $2 \times 4 - 1$
   (l) $2 \times (4 - 1)$
   (m) $2 \times 6 \div (3 - 1)$
   (n) $2 \times (6 \div 3) - 1$
   (o) $2 \times (6 \div 3 - 1)$

2. Prime factorise (a) 56, (b) 39, (c) 74.

3. Find the h.c.f. of
   (a) 8, 12, 14 (b) 18, 42, 66 (c) 20, 24, 30 (d) 16, 24, 32, 160

4. Find the l.c.m. of
   (a) 10, 15 (b) 11, 13 (c) 8, 14, 16 (d) 15, 24, 30

Fractions

Objectives: This chapter:

- explains what is meant by a fraction
- defines the terms 'improper fraction', 'proper fraction' and 'mixed fraction'
- explains how to write fractions in different but equivalent forms
- explains how to simplify fractions by cancelling common factors
- explains how to add, subtract, multiply and divide fractions

2.1 Introduction

The arithmetic of fractions is very important groundwork that must be mastered before topics in algebra such as formulae and equations can be understood. The same techniques that are used to manipulate fractions are used in these more advanced topics. You should use this chapter to ensure that you are confident at handling fractions before moving on to algebra. In all the examples and exercises it is important that you should carry out the calculations without the use of a calculator.

Fractions are numbers such as $\frac{1}{2}$, $\frac{3}{4}$, $\frac{11}{8}$ and so on. In general a fraction is a number of the form $\frac{p}{q}$, where the letters p and q represent whole numbers or integers. The integer q can never be zero because it is never possible to divide by zero.

In any fraction $\frac{p}{q}$ the number p is called the **numerator** and the number q is called the **denominator**.

Key point

$$\text{fraction} = \frac{\text{numerator}}{\text{denominator}} = \frac{p}{q}$$

Suppose that p and q are both positive numbers. If p is less than q, the fraction is said to be a **proper fraction**. So $\frac{1}{2}$ and $\frac{3}{4}$ are proper fractions since the numerator is less than the denominator. If p is greater than or equal to q, the fraction is said to be **improper**. So $\frac{11}{8}$, $\frac{7}{4}$ and $\frac{3}{3}$ are all improper fractions.

If either of p or q is negative, we simply ignore the negative sign when determining whether the fraction is proper or improper. So $-\frac{3}{5}$, $\frac{-7}{21}$ and $\frac{4}{-21}$ are proper fractions, but $\frac{3}{-3}$, $\frac{-8}{2}$ and $-\frac{11}{2}$ are improper.

Note that all proper fractions have a value less than 1.

The denominator of a fraction can take the value 1, as in $\frac{3}{1}$ and $\frac{7}{1}$. In these cases the result is a whole number, 3 and 7.

Self-assessment questions 2.1

1. Explain the terms (a) fraction, (b) improper fraction, (c) proper fraction. In each case give an example of your own.

2. Explain the terms (a) numerator, (b) denominator.

Exercise 2.1

1. Classify each of the following as proper or improper:
   (a) $\frac{9}{17}$ (b) $\frac{-9}{17}$ (c) $\frac{8}{8}$ (d) $-\frac{7}{8}$ (e) $\frac{110}{77}$

2.2 Expressing a fraction in equivalent forms

Given a fraction, we may be able to express it in a different form. For example, you will know that $\frac{1}{2}$ is equivalent to $\frac{2}{4}$. Note that multiplying both numerator and denominator by the same number leaves the value of the fraction unchanged. So, for example,

$$\frac{1}{2} = \frac{1 \times 2}{2 \times 2} = \frac{2}{4}$$

We say that $\frac{1}{2}$ and $\frac{2}{4}$ are **equivalent fractions**. Although they might look different, they have the same value.

Similarly, given the fraction $\frac{8}{12}$ we can divide both numerator and denominator by 4 to obtain

$$\frac{8}{12} = \frac{8/4}{12/4} = \frac{2}{3}$$

so $\frac{8}{12}$ and $\frac{2}{3}$ have the same value and are equivalent fractions.

| Key point | Multiplying or dividing both numerator and denominator of a fraction by the same number produces a fraction having the same value, called an **equivalent fraction**. |

A fraction is in its **simplest form** when there are no factors common to both numerator and denominator. For example, $\frac{5}{12}$ is in its simplest form, but $\frac{3}{6}$ is not since 3 is a factor common to both numerator and denominator. Its simplest form is the equivalent fraction $\frac{1}{2}$.

To express a fraction in its simplest form we look for factors that are common to both the numerator and denominator. This is done by prime factorising both of these. Dividing both the numerator and denominator by any common factors removes them but leaves an equivalent fraction. This is equivalent to cancelling any common factors. For example, to simplify $\frac{4}{6}$ we prime factorise to produce

$$\frac{4}{6} = \frac{2 \times 2}{2 \times 3}$$

Dividing both numerator and denominator by 2 leaves $\frac{2}{3}$. This is equivalent to cancelling the common factor of 2.

WORKED EXAMPLES

2.1   Express $\frac{24}{36}$ in its simplest form.

Solution   We seek factors common to both numerator and denominator. To do this we prime factorise 24 and 36:

Prime factorisation has been described in §1.3.

$$24 = 2 \times 2 \times 2 \times 3 \qquad 36 = 2 \times 2 \times 3 \times 3$$

The factors $2 \times 2 \times 3$ are common to both 24 and 36 and so these may be cancelled. Note that only common factors may be cancelled when simplifying a fraction. Hence

Finding the highest common factor (h.c.f.) of two numbers is detailed in §1.4.

$$\frac{24}{36} = \frac{2 \times 2 \times 2 \times 3}{2 \times 2 \times 3 \times 3} = \frac{2}{3}$$

In its simplest form $\frac{24}{36}$ is $\frac{2}{3}$. In effect we have divided 24 and 36 by 12, which is their h.c.f.

2.2   Express $\frac{49}{21}$ in its simplest form.

Solution   Prime factorising 49 and 21 gives

$$49 = 7 \times 7 \qquad 21 = 3 \times 7$$

Their h.c.f. is 7. Dividing 49 and 21 by 7 gives

$$\frac{49}{21} = \frac{7}{3}$$

Hence the simplest form of $\frac{49}{21}$ is $\frac{7}{3}$.

Before we can start to add and subtract fractions it is necessary to be able to convert fractions into a variety of equivalent forms. Work through the following examples.

WORKED EXAMPLES

2.3   Express $\frac{3}{4}$ as an equivalent fraction having a denominator of 20.

Solution   To achieve a denominator of 20, the existing denominator must be multiplied by 5. To produce an equivalent fraction both numerator and denominator must be multiplied by 5, so

$$\frac{3}{4} = \frac{3 \times 5}{4 \times 5} = \frac{15}{20}$$

2.4   Express 7 as an equivalent fraction with a denominator of 3.

Solution   Note that 7 is the same as the fraction $\frac{7}{1}$. To achieve a denominator of 3, the existing denominator must be multiplied by 3. To produce an equivalent fraction both numerator and denominator must be multiplied by 3, so

$$7 = \frac{7}{1} = \frac{7 \times 3}{1 \times 3} = \frac{21}{3}$$

Self-assessment questions 2.2

1. All integers can be thought of as fractions. True or false?

2. Explain the use of h.c.f. in the simplification of fractions.

3. Give an example of three fractions that are equivalent.

Exercise 2.2

1. Express the following fractions in their simplest form:
    (a) $\frac{18}{27}$ (b) $\frac{12}{20}$ (c) $\frac{15}{45}$ (d) $\frac{25}{80}$ (e) $\frac{15}{60}$
    (f) $\frac{90}{200}$ (g) $\frac{15}{20}$ (h) $\frac{2}{18}$ (i) $\frac{16}{24}$ (j) $\frac{30}{65}$
    (k) $\frac{12}{21}$ (l) $\frac{100}{45}$ (m) $\frac{6}{9}$ (n) $\frac{12}{16}$ (o) $\frac{13}{42}$
    (p) $\frac{13}{39}$ (q) $\frac{11}{33}$ (r) $\frac{14}{30}$ (s) $-\frac{12}{16}$ (t) $\frac{11}{-33}$
    (u) $\frac{-14}{-30}$

2. Express $\frac{3}{4}$ as an equivalent fraction having a denominator of 28.

3. Express 4 as an equivalent fraction with a denominator of 5.

4. Express $\frac{5}{12}$ as an equivalent fraction having a denominator of 36.

5. Express 2 as an equivalent fraction with a denominator of 4.

6. Express 6 as an equivalent fraction with a denominator of 3.

7. Express each of the fractions $\frac{2}{3}$, $\frac{5}{4}$ and $\frac{5}{6}$ as an equivalent fraction with a denominator of 12.

8. Express each of the fractions $\frac{4}{9}$, $\frac{1}{2}$ and $\frac{5}{6}$ as an equivalent fraction with a denominator of 18.

9. Express each of the following numbers as an equivalent fraction with a denominator of 12:
    (a) $\frac{1}{2}$ (b) $\frac{3}{4}$ (c) $\frac{5}{2}$ (d) 5 (e) 4 (f) 12

2.3 Addition and subtraction of fractions

To add and subtract fractions we first rewrite each fraction so that they all have the same denominator. This is known as the **common denominator**. The denominator is chosen to be the lowest common multiple of the original denominators. Then the numerators only are added or subtracted as appropriate, and the result is divided by the common denominator.

WORKED EXAMPLES

2.5   Find $\frac{2}{3} + \frac{5}{4}$.

Solution   The denominators are 3 and 4. The l.c.m. of 3 and 4 is 12. We need to express both fractions with a denominator of 12.

Finding the lowest common multiple (l.c.m.) is detailed in §1.4.

To express $\frac{2}{3}$ with a denominator of 12 we multiply both numerator and denominator by 4. Hence $\frac{2}{3}$ is the same as $\frac{8}{12}$. To express $\frac{5}{4}$ with a denominator of 12 we multiply both numerator and denominator by 3. Hence $\frac{5}{4}$ is the same as $\frac{15}{12}$. So

$$\frac{2}{3} + \frac{5}{4} = \frac{8}{12} + \frac{15}{12} = \frac{8+15}{12} = \frac{23}{12}$$

2.6   Find $\frac{4}{9} - \frac{1}{2} + \frac{5}{6}$.

Solution   The denominators are 9, 2 and 6. Their l.c.m. is 18. Each fraction is expressed with 18 as the denominator:

$$\frac{4}{9} = \frac{8}{18} \qquad \frac{1}{2} = \frac{9}{18} \qquad \frac{5}{6} = \frac{15}{18}$$

Then

$$\frac{4}{9} - \frac{1}{2} + \frac{5}{6} = \frac{8}{18} - \frac{9}{18} + \frac{15}{18} = \frac{8 - 9 + 15}{18} = \frac{14}{18}$$

The fraction $\frac{14}{18}$ can be simplified to $\frac{7}{9}$. Hence

$$\frac{4}{9} - \frac{1}{2} + \frac{5}{6} = \frac{7}{9}$$

2.7   Find $\frac{1}{4} - \frac{5}{9}$.

Solution   The l.c.m. of 4 and 9 is 36. Each fraction is expressed with a denominator of 36. Thus

$$\frac{1}{4} = \frac{9}{36} \qquad \text{and} \qquad \frac{5}{9} = \frac{20}{36}$$

Then

$$\frac{1}{4} - \frac{5}{9} = \frac{9}{36} - \frac{20}{36}$$

$$= \frac{9 - 20}{36}$$

$$= \frac{-11}{36}$$

$$= -\frac{11}{36}$$

Consider the number $2\frac{3}{4}$. This is referred to as a **mixed fraction** because it contains a whole number part, 2, and a fractional part, $\frac{3}{4}$. We can convert this mixed fraction into an improper fraction as follows. Recognise that 2 is equivalent to $\frac{8}{4}$, and so $2\frac{3}{4}$ is $\frac{8}{4} + \frac{3}{4} = \frac{11}{4}$.

The reverse of this process is to convert an improper fraction into a mixed fraction. Consider the improper fraction $\frac{11}{4}$. Now 4 divides into 11 twice leaving a remainder of 3; so $\frac{11}{4} = 2$ remainder 3, which we write as $2\frac{3}{4}$.

WORKED EXAMPLE

2.8 (a) Express $4\frac{2}{5}$ as an improper fraction.

(b) Find $4\frac{2}{5} + \frac{1}{3}$.

Solution (a) $4\frac{2}{5}$ is a mixed fraction. Note that $4\frac{2}{5}$ is equal to $4 + \frac{2}{5}$. We can write 4 as the equivalent fraction $\frac{20}{5}$. Therefore

$$4\frac{2}{5} = \frac{20}{5} + \frac{2}{5}$$

$$= \frac{22}{5}$$

(b) $4\frac{2}{5} + \frac{1}{3} = \frac{22}{5} + \frac{1}{3}$

$$= \frac{66}{15} + \frac{5}{15}$$

$$= \frac{71}{15}$$

Self-assessment question 2.3

1. Explain the use of l.c.m. when adding and subtracting fractions.

Exercise 2.3

MyMathLab

1. Find
   (a) $\frac{1}{4} + \frac{2}{3}$ (b) $\frac{3}{5} + \frac{5}{3}$ (c) $\frac{12}{14} - \frac{2}{7}$

   (d) $\frac{3}{7} - \frac{1}{2} + \frac{2}{21}$ (e) $1\frac{1}{2} + \frac{4}{9}$

   (f) $2\frac{1}{4} - 1\frac{1}{3} + \frac{1}{2}$ (g) $\frac{10}{15} - 1\frac{2}{5} + \frac{8}{3}$

   (h) $\frac{9}{10} - \frac{7}{16} + \frac{1}{2} - \frac{2}{5}$

2. Find
   (a) $\frac{7}{8} + \frac{1}{3}$ (b) $\frac{1}{2} - \frac{3}{4}$ (c) $\frac{3}{5} + \frac{2}{3} + \frac{1}{2}$

   (d) $\frac{3}{8} + \frac{1}{3} + \frac{1}{4}$ (e) $\frac{2}{3} - \frac{4}{7}$

   (f) $\frac{1}{11} - \frac{1}{2}$ (g) $\frac{3}{11} - \frac{5}{8}$

3. Express as improper fractions:

(a) $2\frac{1}{2}$ (b) $3\frac{2}{3}$ (c) $10\frac{1}{4}$ (d) $5\frac{2}{7}$

(e) $6\frac{2}{9}$ (f) $11\frac{1}{3}$ (g) $15\frac{1}{2}$ (h) $13\frac{3}{4}$

(i) $12\frac{1}{11}$ (j) $13\frac{2}{3}$ (k) $56\frac{1}{2}$

4. Without using a calculator express these improper fractions as mixed fractions:

(a) $\frac{10}{3}$ (b) $\frac{7}{2}$ (c) $\frac{15}{4}$ (d) $\frac{25}{6}$

2.4 Multiplication of fractions

The product of two or more fractions is found by multiplying their numerators to form a new numerator, and then multiplying their denominators to form a new denominator.

WORKED EXAMPLES

2.9   Find $\frac{4}{9} \times \frac{3}{8}$.

Solution   The numerators are multiplied: $4 \times 3 = 12$. The denominators are multiplied: $9 \times 8 = 72$. Hence

$$\frac{4}{9} \times \frac{3}{8} = \frac{12}{72}$$

This may now be expressed in its simplest form:

$$\frac{12}{72} = \frac{1}{6}$$

Hence

$$\frac{4}{9} \times \frac{3}{8} = \frac{1}{6}$$

An alternative, but equivalent, method is to cancel any factors common to both numerator and denominator at the outset:

$$\frac{4}{9} \times \frac{3}{8} = \frac{4 \times 3}{9 \times 8}$$

A factor of 4 is common to the 4 and the 8. Hence

$$\frac{4 \times 3}{9 \times 8} = \frac{1 \times 3}{9 \times 2}$$

A factor of 3 is common to the 3 and the 9. Hence

$$\frac{1 \times 3}{9 \times 2} = \frac{1 \times 1}{3 \times 2} = \frac{1}{6}$$

2.10   Find $\frac{12}{25} \times \frac{2}{7} \times \frac{10}{9}$.

Solution   We cancel factors common to both numerator and denominator. A factor of 5 is common to 10 and 25. Cancelling this gives

$$\frac{12}{25} \times \frac{2}{7} \times \frac{10}{9} = \frac{12}{5} \times \frac{2}{7} \times \frac{2}{9}$$

A factor of 3 is common to 12 and 9. Cancelling this gives

$$\frac{12}{5} \times \frac{2}{7} \times \frac{2}{9} = \frac{4}{5} \times \frac{2}{7} \times \frac{2}{3}$$

There are no more common factors. Hence

$$\frac{12}{25} \times \frac{2}{7} \times \frac{10}{9} = \frac{4}{5} \times \frac{2}{7} \times \frac{2}{3} = \frac{16}{105}$$

2.11   Find $\frac{3}{4}$ of $\frac{5}{9}$.

Recall that 'of' means multiply.

Solution $\frac{3}{4}$ of $\frac{5}{9}$ is the same as $\frac{3}{4} \times \frac{5}{9}$. Cancelling a factor of 3 from numerator and denominator gives $\frac{1}{4} \times \frac{5}{3}$, that is $\frac{5}{12}$. Hence $\frac{3}{4}$ of $\frac{5}{9}$ is $\frac{5}{12}$.

2.12   Find $\frac{5}{6}$ of 70.

Solution   We can write 70 as $\frac{70}{1}$. So

$$\frac{5}{6} \text{ of } 70 = \frac{5}{6} \times \frac{70}{1} = \frac{5}{3} \times \frac{35}{1} = \frac{175}{3} = 58\frac{1}{3}$$

2.13   Find $2\frac{7}{8} \times \frac{2}{3}$.

Solution   In this example the first fraction is a mixed fraction. We convert it to an improper fraction before performing the multiplication. Note that $2\frac{7}{8} = \frac{23}{8}$. Then

$$\frac{23}{8} \times \frac{2}{3} = \frac{23}{4} \times \frac{1}{3}$$

$$= \frac{23}{12}$$

$$= 1\frac{11}{12}$$

Self-assessment question 2.4

1. Describe how to multiply fractions together.

Exercise 2.4

1. Evaluate

   (a) $\frac{2}{3} \times \frac{6}{7}$ (b) $\frac{8}{15} \times \frac{25}{32}$ (c) $\frac{1}{4} \times \frac{8}{9}$

   (d) $\frac{16}{17} \times \frac{34}{48}$ (e) $2 \times \frac{3}{5} \times \frac{5}{12}$

   (f) $2\frac{1}{3} \times 1\frac{1}{4}$ (g) $1\frac{3}{4} \times 2\frac{1}{2}$

   (h) $\frac{3}{4} \times 1\frac{1}{2} \times 3\frac{1}{2}$

2. Evaluate

   (a) $\frac{2}{3}$ of $\frac{3}{4}$ (b) $\frac{4}{7}$ of $\frac{21}{30}$

   (c) $\frac{9}{10}$ of 80 (d) $\frac{6}{7}$ of 42

3. Is $\frac{3}{4}$ of $\frac{12}{15}$ the same as $\frac{12}{15}$ of $\frac{3}{4}$?

4. Find

   (a) $-\frac{1}{3} \times \frac{5}{7}$ (b) $\frac{3}{4} \times -\frac{1}{2}$

   (c) $\left(-\frac{5}{8}\right) \times \frac{8}{11}$ (d) $\left(-\frac{2}{3}\right) \times \left(-\frac{15}{7}\right)$

5. Find

   (a) $5\frac{1}{2} \times \frac{1}{2}$ (b) $3\frac{3}{4} \times \frac{1}{3}$

   (c) $\frac{2}{3} \times 5\frac{1}{9}$ (d) $\frac{3}{4} \times 11\frac{1}{2}$

6. Find

   (a) $\frac{3}{5}$ of $11\frac{1}{4}$ (b) $\frac{2}{3}$ of $15\frac{1}{2}$

   (c) $\frac{1}{4}$ of $-8\frac{1}{3}$

2.5 Division by a fraction

To divide one fraction by another fraction, we invert the second fraction and then multiply. When we invert a fraction we interchange the numerator and denominator.

WORKED EXAMPLES

2.14   Find $\frac{6}{25} \div \frac{2}{5}$.

Solution   We invert $\frac{2}{5}$ to obtain $\frac{5}{2}$. Multiplication is then performed. So

$$\frac{6}{25} \div \frac{2}{5} = \frac{6}{25} \times \frac{5}{2} = \frac{3}{25} \times \frac{5}{1} = \frac{3}{5} \times \frac{1}{1} = \frac{3}{5}$$

2.15   Evaluate (a) $1\frac{1}{3} \div \frac{8}{3}$,   (b) $\frac{20}{21} \div \frac{5}{7}$.

Solution   (a)   First we express $1\frac{1}{3}$ as an improper fraction:

$$1\frac{1}{3} = 1 + \frac{1}{3} = \frac{3}{3} + \frac{1}{3} = \frac{4}{3}$$

So we calculate

$$\frac{4}{3} \div \frac{8}{3} = \frac{4}{3} \times \frac{3}{8} = \frac{4}{8} = \frac{1}{2}$$

Hence

$$1\frac{1}{3} \div \frac{8}{3} = \frac{1}{2}$$

(b) $\dfrac{20}{21} \div \dfrac{5}{7} = \dfrac{20}{21} \times \dfrac{7}{5} = \dfrac{4}{21} \times \dfrac{7}{1} = \dfrac{4}{3}$

Self-assessment question 2.5

1.   Explain the process of division by a fraction.

Exercise 2.5

MyMathLab Global

1. Evaluate

(a) $\dfrac{3}{4} \div \dfrac{1}{8}$

(b) $\dfrac{8}{9} \div \dfrac{4}{3}$

(c) $\dfrac{-2}{7} \div \dfrac{4}{21}$

(d) $\dfrac{9}{4} \div 1\dfrac{1}{2}$

(e) $\dfrac{5}{6} \div \dfrac{5}{12}$

(f) $\dfrac{99}{100} \div 1\dfrac{4}{5}$

(g) $3\dfrac{1}{4} \div 1\dfrac{1}{8}$

(h) $\left(2\dfrac{1}{4} \div \dfrac{3}{4} \right) \times 2$

(i) $2\dfrac{1}{4} \div \left(\dfrac{3}{4} \times 2 \right)$

(j) $6\dfrac{1}{4} \div 2\dfrac{1}{2} + 5$

(k) $6\dfrac{1}{4} \div \left(2\dfrac{1}{2} + 5 \right)$

1. Evaluate

(a) $\dfrac{3}{4} + \dfrac{1}{6}$

(b) $\dfrac{2}{3} + \dfrac{3}{5} - \dfrac{1}{6}$

(c) $\dfrac{5}{7} - \dfrac{2}{3}$

(d) $2\dfrac{1}{3} - \dfrac{9}{10}$

(e) $5\dfrac{1}{4} + 3\dfrac{1}{6}$

(f) $\dfrac{9}{8} - \dfrac{7}{6} + 1$

(g) $\dfrac{5}{6} - \dfrac{5}{3} + \dfrac{5}{4}$

(h) $\dfrac{4}{5} + \dfrac{1}{3} - \dfrac{3}{4}$

2. Evaluate

(a) $\dfrac{4}{7} \times \dfrac{21}{32}$

(b) $\dfrac{5}{6} \times \dfrac{8}{15}$

(c) $\dfrac{3}{11} \times \dfrac{20}{21}$

(d) $\dfrac{9}{14} \times \dfrac{8}{18}$

(e) $\dfrac{5}{4} \div \dfrac{10}{13}$

(f) $\dfrac{7}{16} \div \dfrac{21}{32}$

(g) $\dfrac{-24}{25} \div \dfrac{51}{50}$

(h) $\dfrac{45}{81} \div \dfrac{25}{27}$

3. Evaluate the following expressions using the BODMAS rule:

(a) $\dfrac{1}{2} + \dfrac{1}{3} \times 2$

(b) $\dfrac{3}{4} \times \dfrac{2}{3} + \dfrac{1}{4}$

(c) $\dfrac{5}{6} \div \dfrac{2}{3} + \dfrac{3}{4}$

(d) $\left(\dfrac{2}{3} + \dfrac{1}{4} \right) \div 4 + \dfrac{3}{5}$

(e) $\left(\dfrac{4}{3} - \dfrac{2}{5} \times \dfrac{1}{3} \right) \times \dfrac{1}{4} + \dfrac{1}{2}$

(f) $\dfrac{3}{4}$ of $\left(1 + \dfrac{2}{3} \right)$

(g) $\dfrac{2}{3}$ of $\dfrac{1}{2} + 1$

(h) $\dfrac{1}{5} \times \dfrac{2}{3} + \dfrac{2}{5} \div \dfrac{4}{5}$

4. Express in their simplest form:

(a) $\dfrac{21}{84}$

(b) $\dfrac{6}{80}$

(c) $\dfrac{34}{85}$

(d) $\dfrac{22}{143}$

(e) $\dfrac{69}{253}$

Decimal fractions

Objectives: This chapter:

- ▪ revises the decimal number system
- ▪ shows how to write a number to a given number of significant figures
- ▪ shows how to write a number to a given number of decimal places

3.1 Decimal numbers

Consider the whole number 478. We can regard it as the sum

$$400 + 70 + 8$$

In this way we see that, in the number 478, the 8 represents eight ones, or 8 units, the 7 represents seven tens, or 70, and the number 4 represents four hundreds or 400. Thus we have the system of hundreds, tens and units familiar from early years in school. All whole numbers can be thought of in this way.

When we wish to deal with proper fractions and mixed fractions, we extend the hundreds, tens and units system as follows. A **decimal point**, '.', marks the end of the whole number part, and the numbers that follow it, to the right, form the fractional part.

A number immediately to the right of the decimal point, that is in the **first decimal place**, represents tenths, so

$$0.1 = \frac{1}{10}$$

$$0.2 = \frac{2}{10} \quad \text{or} \quad \frac{1}{5}$$

$$0.3 = \frac{3}{10} \quad \text{and so on}$$

Note that when there are no whole numbers involved it is usual to write a zero in front of the decimal point, thus, .2 would be written 0.2.

WORKED EXAMPLE

3.1 Express the following decimal numbers as proper fractions in their simplest form

(a) 0.4   (b) 0.5   (c) 0.6

Solution The first number after the decimal point represents tenths.

(a) $0.4 = \frac{4}{10}$, which simplifies to $\frac{2}{5}$

(b) $0.5 = \frac{5}{10}$ or simply $\frac{1}{2}$

(c) $0.6 = \frac{6}{10} = \frac{3}{5}$

Frequently we will deal with numbers having a whole number part and a fractional part. Thus

$$5.2 = 5 \text{ units} + 2 \text{ tenths}$$

$$= 5 + \frac{2}{10}$$

$$= 5 + \frac{1}{5}$$

$$= 5\frac{1}{5}$$

Similarly,

$$175.8 = 175\frac{8}{10} = 175\frac{4}{5}$$

Numbers in the second position after the decimal point, or the **second decimal place**, represent hundredths, so

$$0.01 = \frac{1}{100}$$

$$0.02 = \frac{2}{100} \quad \text{or} \quad \frac{1}{50}$$

$$0.03 = \frac{3}{100} \quad \text{and so on}$$

Consider 0.25. We can think of this as

$$0.25 = 0.2 + 0.05$$

$$= \frac{2}{10} + \frac{5}{100}$$

$$= \frac{25}{100}$$

We see that 0.25 is equivalent to $\frac{25}{100}$, which in its simplest form is $\frac{1}{4}$.

In fact we can regard any numbers occupying the first two decimal places as hundredths, so that

$$0.25 = \frac{25}{100} \quad \text{or simply} \quad \frac{1}{4}$$

$$0.50 = \frac{50}{100} \quad \text{or} \quad \frac{1}{2}$$

$$0.75 = \frac{75}{100} = \frac{3}{4}$$

WORKED EXAMPLES

3.2   Express the following decimal numbers as proper fractions in their simplest form:

(a) 0.35   (b) 0.56   (c) 0.68

Solution   The first two decimal places represent hundredths:

(a) $0.35 = \frac{35}{100} = \frac{7}{20}$

(b) $0.56 = \frac{56}{100} = \frac{14}{25}$

(c) $0.68 = \frac{68}{100} = \frac{17}{25}$

3.3   Express 37.25 as a mixed fraction in its simplest form.

Solution $37.25 = 37 + 0.25$

$$= 37 + \frac{25}{100}$$

$$= 37 + \frac{1}{4}$$

$$= 37\frac{1}{4}$$

Numbers in the third position after the decimal point, or **third decimal place**, represent thousandths, so

$$0.001 = \frac{1}{1000}$$

$$0.002 = \frac{2}{1000} \quad \text{or} \quad \frac{1}{500}$$

$$0.003 = \frac{3}{1000} \quad \text{and so on}$$

In fact we can regard any numbers occupying the first three positions after the decimal point as thousandths, so that

$$0.356 = \frac{356}{1000} \quad \text{or} \quad \frac{89}{250}$$

$$0.015 = \frac{15}{1000} \quad \text{or} \quad \frac{3}{200}$$

$$0.075 = \frac{75}{1000} = \frac{3}{40}$$

WORKED EXAMPLE

3.4   Write each of the following as a decimal number:

(a) $\frac{3}{10} + \frac{7}{100}$ (b) $\frac{8}{10} + \frac{3}{1000}$

Solution

(a) $\frac{3}{10} + \frac{7}{100} = 0.3 + 0.07 = 0.37$

(b) $\frac{8}{10} + \frac{3}{1000} = 0.8 + 0.003 = 0.803$

You will normally use a calculator to add, subtract, multiply and divide decimal numbers. Generally the more decimal places used, the more accurately we can state a number. This idea is developed in the next section.

Self-assessment questions 3.1

1. State which is the largest and which is the smallest of the following numbers:
   23.001, 23.0, 23.00001, 23.0008, 23.01

2. Which is the largest of the following numbers?
   0.1, 0.02, 0.003, 0.0004, 0.00005

Exercise 3.1

MyMathLab Global

1. Express the following decimal numbers as proper fractions in their simplest form:
   (a) 0.7 (b) 0.8 (c) 0.9

2. Express the following decimal numbers as proper fractions in their simplest form:
   (a) 0.55 (b) 0.158 (c) 0.98
   (d) 0.099

3. Express each of the following as a mixed fraction in its simplest form:
   (a) 4.6 (b) 5.2 (c) 8.05 (d) 11.59
   (e) 121.09

4. Write each of the following as a decimal number:
   (a) $\frac{6}{10} + \frac{9}{100} + \frac{7}{1000}$ (b) $\frac{8}{100} + \frac{3}{1000}$
   (c) $\frac{17}{1000} + \frac{5}{10}$

3.2 Significant figures and decimal places

The accuracy with which we state a number often depends upon the context in which the number is being used. The volume of a petrol tank is usually given to the nearest litre. It is of no practical use to give such a volume to the nearest cubic centimetre.

When writing a number we often give the accuracy by stating the **number of significant figures** or the **number of decimal places** used. These terms are now explained.

Significant figures

Suppose we are asked to write down the number nearest to 857 using at most two non-zero digits, or numbers. We would write 860. This number is nearer to 857 than any other number with two non-zero digits. We say that 857 to 2 **significant figures** is 860. The words 'significant figures' are usually abbreviated to s.f. Because 860 is larger than 857 we say that the 857 has been **rounded up** to 860.

To write a number to three significant figures we can use no more than three non-zero digits. For example, the number closest to 1784 which has no more than three non-zero digits is 1780. We say that 1784 to 3 significant figures is 1780. In this case, because 1780 is less than 1784 we say that 1784 has been **rounded down** to 1780.

WORKED EXAMPLES

3.5 Write down the number nearest to 86 using only one non-zero digit. Has 86 been rounded up or down?

Solution   The number 86 written to one significant figure is 90. This number is nearer to 86 than any other number having only one non-zero digit. 86 has been rounded up to 90.

3.6   Write down the number nearest to 999 which uses only one non-zero digit.

Solution   The number 999 to one significant figure is 1000. This number is nearer to 999 than any other number having only one non-zero digit.

We now explain the process of writing to a given number of significant figures.

When asked to write a number to, say, three significant figures, 3 s.f., the first step is to look at the first four digits. If asked to write a number to two significant figures we look at the first three digits and so on. We always look at one more digit than the number of significant figures required.

For example, to write 6543.19 to 2 s.f. we would consider the number 6540.00; the digits 3, 1 and 9 are effectively ignored. The next step is to round up or down. If the final digit is a 5 or more then we round up by increasing the previous digit by 1. If the final digit is 4 or less we round down by leaving the previous digit unchanged. Hence when considering 6543.19 to 2 s.f., the 4 in the third place means that we round down to 6500.

To write 23865 to 3 s.f. we would consider the number 23860. The next step is to increase the 8 to a 9. Thus 23865 is rounded up to 23900.

Zeros at the beginning of a number are ignored. To write 0.004693 to 2 s.f. we would first consider the number 0.00469. Note that the zeros at the beginning of the number have not been counted. We then round the 6 to a 7, producing 0.0047.

The following examples illustrate the process.

WORKED EXAMPLES

3.7   Write 36.482 to 3 s.f.

Solution   We consider the first four digits, that is 36.48. The final digit is 8 and so we round up 36.48 to 36.5. To 3 s.f. 36.482 is 36.5.

3.8   Write 1.0049 to 4 s.f.

Solution   To write to 4 s.f. we consider the first five digits, that is 1.0049. The final digit is a 9 and so 1.0049 is rounded up to 1.005.

3.9   Write 695.3 to 2 s.f.

Solution   We consider 695. The final digit is a 5 and so we round up. We cannot round up the 9 to a 10 and so the 69 is rounded up to 70. Hence to 2 s.f. the number is 700.

3.10   Write 0.0473 to 1 s.f.

Solution   We do not count the initial zeros and consider 0.047. The final digit tells us to round up. Hence to 1 s.f. we have 0.05.

3.11   A number is given to 2 s.f. as 67.

(a) What is the maximum value the number could have?
(b) What is the minimum value the number could have?

Solution   (a) To 2 s.f. 67.5 is 68. Any number just below 67.5, for example 67.49 or 67.499, to 2 s.f. is 67. Hence the maximum value of the number is 67.4999....

(b) To 2 s.f. 66.4999... is 66. However, 66.5 to 2 s.f. is 67. The minimum value of the number is thus 66.5.

Decimal places

When asked to write a number to 3 decimal places (3 d.p.) we consider the first 4 decimal places, that is numbers after the decimal point. If asked to write to 2 d.p. we consider the first 3 decimal places and so on. If the final digit is 5 or more we round up, otherwise we round down.

WORKED EXAMPLES

3.12   Write 63.4261 to 2 d.p.

Solution   We consider the number to 3 d.p., that is 63.426. The final digit is 6 and so we round up 63.426 to 63.43. Hence 63.4261 to 2 d.p. is 63.43.

3.13   Write 1.97 to 1 d.p.

Solution   In order to write to 1 d.p. we consider the number to 2 d.p., that is we consider 1.97. The final digit is a 7 and so we round up. The 9 cannot be rounded up and so we look at 1.9. This can be rounded up to 2.0. Hence 1.97 to 1 d.p. is 2.0. Note that it is crucial to write 2.0 and not simply 2, as this shows that the number is written to 1 d.p.

3.14   Write −6.0439 to 2 d.p.

Solution   We consider −6.043. As the final digit is a 3 the number is rounded down to −6.04.

Self-assessment questions 3.2

1. Explain the meaning of 'significant figures'.

2. Explain the process of writing a number to so many decimal places.

Exercise 3.2

1. Write to 3 s.f.
   (a) 6962   (b) 70.406   (c) 0.0123
   (d) 0.010991   (e) 45.607   (f) 2345

2. Write 65.999 to
   (a) 4 s.f.   (b) 3 s.f.   (c) 2 s.f.
   (d) 1 s.f.   (e) 2 d.p.   (f) 1 d.p.

3. Write 9.99 to
   (a) 1 s.f.   (b) 1 d.p.

4. Write 65.4555 to
   (a) 3 d.p.   (b) 2 d.p.   (c) 1 d.p.
   (d) 5 s.f.   (e) 4 s.f.   (f) 3 s.f.   (g) 2 s.f.
   (h) 1 s.f.

1. Express the following numbers as proper fractions in their simplest form:
   (a) 0.74   (b) 0.96   (c) 0.05   (d) 0.25

2. Express each of the following as a mixed fraction in its simplest form:
   (a) 2.5   (b) 3.25   (c) 3.125   (d) 6.875

3. Write each of the following as a decimal number:
   (a) $\frac{3}{10} + \frac{1}{100} + \frac{7}{1000}$ (b) $\frac{5}{1000} + \frac{9}{100}$ (c) $\frac{4}{1000} + \frac{9}{10}$

4. Write 0.09846 to (a) 1 d.p, (b) 2 s.f., (c) 1 s.f.

5. Write 9.513 to (a) 3 s.f., (b) 2 s.f., (c) 1 s.f.

6. Write 19.96 to (a) 1 d.p., (b) 2 s.f., (c) 1 s.f.

Percentage and ratio

4

Objectives: This chapter:

- explains the terms 'percentage' and 'ratio'
- shows how to perform calculations using percentages and ratios
- explains how to calculate the percentage change in a quantity

4.1 Percentage

In everyday life we come across percentages regularly. During sales periods shops offer discounts – for example, we might hear expressions like 'everything reduced by 50%'. Students often receive examination marks in the form of percentages – for example, to achieve a pass grade in a university examination, a student may be required to score at least 40%. Banks and building societies charge interest on loans, and the interest rate quoted is usually given as a percentage, for example 4.75%. Percentages also provide a way of comparing two or more quantities. For example, suppose we want to know which is the better mark: 40 out of 70, or 125 out of 200? By expressing these marks as percentages we will be able to answer this question.

Consequently an understanding of what a percentage is, and an ability to perform calculations involving percentages, are not only useful in mathematical applications, but also essential life skills.

Most calculators have a percentage button and we will illustrate the use of this later in the chapter. However, be aware that different calculators work in different and often confusing ways. Misleading results can be obtained if you do not know how to use your calculator correctly. So it is better if you are not over-reliant on your calculator and instead understand the principles behind percentage calculations.

Fundamentally, a **percentage** is a fraction whose denominator is 100. In fact you can think of the phrase 'per cent' meaning 'out of 100'. We use the symbol % to represent a percentage, as earlier. The following three fractions all have a denominator of 100, and are expressed as percentages as shown:

$$\frac{17}{100} \quad \text{may be expressed as} \quad 17\%$$

$$\frac{50}{100} \quad \text{may be expressed as} \quad 50\%$$

$$\frac{3}{100} \quad \text{may be expressed as} \quad 3\%$$

WORKED EXAMPLE

4.1   Express $\frac{19}{100}$, $\frac{35}{100}$ and $\frac{17.5}{100}$ as percentages.

Solution   All of these fractions have a denominator of 100. So it is straightforward to write down their percentage form:

$$\frac{19}{100} = 19\% \qquad \frac{35}{100} = 35\% \qquad \frac{17.5}{100} = 17.5\%$$

Sometimes it is necessary to convert a fraction whose denominator is not 100, for example $\frac{2}{5}$, into a percentage. This could be done by expressing the fraction as an equivalent fraction with denominator 100, as was explained in Section 2.2 on page 15. However, with calculators readily available, the calculation can be done as follows.

We can use the calculator to divide the numerator of the fraction by the denominator. The answer is then multiplied by 100. The resulting number is the required percentage. So, to convert $\frac{2}{5}$ we perform the following key strokes:

$$2 \div 5 \times 100 = 40$$

and so $\frac{2}{5} = 40\%$. You should check this now using your own calculator,

---

Key point   To convert a fraction to a percentage, divide the numerator by the denominator, multiply by 100 and then label the result as a percentage.

WORKED EXAMPLES

4.2   Convert $\frac{5}{8}$ into a percentage.

Solution   Using the method described above we find

$$5 \div 8 \times 100 = 62.5$$

Labelling the answer as a percentage, we see that $\frac{5}{8}$ is equivalent to 62.5%.

4.3   Bill scores $\frac{13}{17}$ in a test. In a different test, Mary scores $\frac{14}{19}$. Express the scores as percentages, and thereby make a comparison of the two marks.

Solution   Use your calculator to perform the division and then multiply the result by 100.

Bill's score: $13 \div 17 \times 100 = 76.5$ (1 d.p.)

Mary's score: $14 \div 19 \times 100 = 73.7$ (1 d.p.)

So we see that Bill scores 76.5% and Mary scores 73.7%. Notice that in these percentage forms it is easy to compare the two marks. We see that Bill has achieved the higher score. Making easy comparisons like this is one of the reasons why percentages are used so frequently.

We have seen that percentages are fractions with a denominator of 100, so that, for example, $\frac{19}{100} = 19\%$. Sometimes a fraction may be given not as a numerator divided by a denominator, but in its decimal form. For example, the decimal form of $\frac{19}{100}$ is 0.19. To convert a decimal fraction into a percentage we simply multiply by 100. So

$$0.19 = 0.19 \times 100\% = 19\%$$

Key point   To convert a decimal fraction to a percentage, multiply by 100 and then label the result as a percentage.

We may also want to reverse the process. Frequently in business calculations involving formulae for interest it is necessary to express a percentage in its decimal form. To convert a percentage to its equivalent decimal form we divide the percentage by 100. Alternatively, using a calculator, input the percentage and press the % button, to convert the percentage to its decimal form.

WORKED EXAMPLE

4.4   Express 50% as a decimal.

Solution   We divide the percentage by 100:

$$50 \div 100 = 0.5$$

So 50% is equivalent to 0.5. To see why this is the case, remember that 'per cent' literally means 'out of 100' so 50% means 50 out of 100, or $\frac{50}{100}$, or in its simplest form 0.5.

Alternatively, using a calculator, the key strokes

50 **%**

should give 0.5. Check whether you can do this on your calculator.

| **Key point** | To convert a percentage to its equivalent decimal fraction form, divide by 100. |

WORKED EXAMPLE

4.5   Express 17.5% as a decimal.

Solution   We divide the percentage by 100:

$$17.5 \div 100 = 0.175$$

So 17.5% is equivalent to 0.175. Now check you can obtain the same result using the percentage button on your calculator.

Some percentages appear so frequently in everyday life that it is useful to learn their fraction and decimal fraction equivalent forms.

| **Key point** | $10\% = 0.1 = \frac{1}{10}$ $25\% = 0.25 = \frac{1}{4}$ |
| | $50\% = 0.5 = \frac{1}{2}$ $75\% = 0.75 = \frac{3}{4}$ $100\% = 1$ |

Recall from Section 1.2 that 'of' means multiply.

We are often asked to calculate a percentage of a quantity: for example, find 17.5% of 160 or 10% of 95. Such calculations arise when finding discounts on prices. Since $17.5\% = \frac{17.5}{100}$ we find

$$17.5\% \text{ of } 160 = \frac{17.5}{100} \times 160 = 28$$

and since $10\% = 0.1$ we may write

$$10\% \text{ of } 95 = 0.1 \times 95 = 9.5$$

Alternatively, the percentage button on a calculator can be used: check you can use your calculator correctly by verifying

17.5 **%** $\times 160 = 28$

Because finding 10% of a quantity is equivalent to dividing by 10, it is easy to find 10% by moving the decimal point one place to the left.

10 **%** $\times 95 = 9.5$

4.6   Calculate 27% of 90.

Solution   Using a calculator

$$27 \boxed{\%} \times 90 = 24.3$$

4.7   Calculate 100% of 6.

Solution

$$100 \boxed{\%} \times 6 = 6$$

Observe that 100% of a number is simply the number itself.

4.8   A deposit of £750 increases by 9%. Calculate the resulting deposit.

Solution   We use a calculator to find 9% of 750. This is the amount by which the deposit has increased. Then

$$9 \boxed{\%} \times 750 = 67.50$$

The deposit has increased by £67.50. The resulting deposit is therefore $750 + 67.5 = £817.50$.

Alternatively we may perform the calculation as follows. The original deposit represents 100%. The deposit increases by 9% to 109% of the original. So the resulting deposit is 109% of £750:

$$109 \boxed{\%} \times 750 = £817.50$$

4.9   A television set is advertised at £315. The retailer offers a 10% discount. How much do you pay for the television?

Solution   10% of 315 = 31.50

The discount is £31.50 and so the cost is $315 - 31.5 = £283.50$.

Alternatively we can note that since the discount is 10%, then the selling price is 90% of the advertised price:

$$90 \boxed{\%} \times 315 = 283.50$$

Performing the calculation in the two ways will increase your understanding of percentages and serve as a check.

When a quantity changes, it is sometimes useful to calculate the **percentage change**. For example, suppose a worker earns £14,500 in the current year, and last year earned £13,650. The actual amount earned has changed by 14,500 − 13,650 = £850. The percentage change is calculated from the formula:

$$\text{percentage change} = \frac{\text{change}}{\text{original value}} \times 100 = \frac{\text{new value} - \text{original value}}{\text{original value}} \times 100$$

If the change is positive, then there has been an increase in the measured quantity. If the change is negative, then there has been a decrease in the quantity.

WORKED EXAMPLES

4.10   A worker's earnings increase from £13,650 to £14,500. Calculate the percentage change.

Solution

$$\text{percentage change} = \frac{\text{new value} - \text{original value}}{\text{original value}} \times 100$$

$$= \frac{14,500 - 13,650}{13,650} \times 100$$

$$= 6.23$$

The worker's earnings increased by 6.23%.

4.11   A microwave oven is reduced in price from £149.95 to £135. Calculate the percentage change in price.

Solution

$$\text{percentage change} = \frac{\text{new value} - \text{original value}}{\text{original value}} \times 100$$

$$= \frac{135 - 149.95}{149.95} \times 100$$

$$= -9.97$$

The negative result is indicative of the price decrease. The percentage change in price is approximately −10%.

Self-assessment question 4.1

1. Give one reason why it is sometimes useful to express fractions as percentages.

Exercise 4.1

MyMathLab

1. Calculate 23% of 124.

2. Express the following as percentages:

   (a) $\dfrac{9}{11}$ (b) $\dfrac{15}{20}$ (c) $\dfrac{9}{10}$ (d) $\dfrac{45}{50}$ (e) $\dfrac{75}{90}$

3. Express $\frac{13}{12}$ as a percentage.

4. Calculate 217% of 500.

5. A worker earns £400 a week. She receives a 6% increase. Calculate her new weekly wage.

6. A debt of £1200 is decreased by 17%. Calculate the remaining debt.

7. Express the following percentages as decimals:

   (a) 50% (b) 36% (c) 75%
   (d) 100% (e) 12.5%

8. A compact disc player normally priced at £256 is reduced in a sale by 20%. Calculate the sale price.

9. A bank deposit earns 7.5% interest in one year. Calculate the interest earned on a deposit of £15,000.

10. The cost of a car is increased from £6950 to £7495. Calculate the percentage change in price.

11. During a sale, a washing machine is reduced in price from £525 to £399. Calculate the percentage change in price.

4.2 Ratio

Ratios are simply an alternative way of expressing fractions. Consider the problem of dividing £200 between two people, Ann and Bill, in the ratio of $7:3$. This means that Ann receives £7 for every £3 that Bill receives. So every £10 is divided as £7 to Ann and £3 to Bill. Thus Ann receives $\frac{7}{10}$ of the money. Now $\frac{7}{10}$ of £200 is $\frac{7}{10} \times 200 = 140$. So Ann receives £140 and Bill receives £60.

WORKED EXAMPLE

4.12   Divide 170 in the ratio $3:2$.

Solution   A ratio of $3:2$ means that every 5 parts are split as 3 and 2. That is, the first number is $\frac{3}{5}$ of the total; the second number is $\frac{2}{5}$ of the total. So

$$\frac{3}{5} \text{ of } 170 = \frac{3}{5} \times 170 = 102$$

$$\frac{2}{5} \text{ of } 170 = \frac{2}{5} \times 170 = 68$$

The number is divided into 102 and 68.

Note from Worked Example 4.12 that to split a number in a given ratio we first find the total number of parts. The total number of parts is found by adding the numbers in the ratio. For example, if the ratio is given as $m:n$, the total number of parts is $m+n$. Then these $m+n$ parts are split into two with the first number being $\frac{m}{m+n}$ of the total, and the second number being $\frac{n}{m+n}$ of the total. Compare this with Worked Example 4.12.

WORKED EXAMPLE

4.13   Divide 250 cm in the ratio $1:3:4$.

Solution   Every 8 cm is divided into 1 cm, 3 cm and 4 cm. Thus the first length is $\frac{1}{8}$ of the total, the second length is $\frac{3}{8}$ of the total, and the third length is $\frac{4}{8}$ of the total:

$$\frac{1}{8} \text{ of } 250 = \frac{1}{8} \times 250 = 31.25$$

$$\frac{3}{8} \text{ of } 250 = \frac{3}{8} \times 250 = 93.75$$

$$\frac{4}{8} \text{ of } 250 = \frac{4}{8} \times 250 = 125$$

The 250 cm length is divided into 31.25 cm, 93.75 cm and 125 cm.

Ratios can be written in different ways. The ratio $3:2$ can also be written as $6:4$. This is clear if we note that $6:4$ is a total of 10 parts split as $\frac{6}{10}$ and $\frac{4}{10}$ of the total. Since $\frac{6}{10}$ is equivalent to $\frac{3}{5}$, and $\frac{4}{10}$ is equivalent to $\frac{2}{5}$, we see that $6:4$ is equivalent to $3:2$.

Generally, any ratio can be expressed as an equivalent ratio by multiplying or dividing each term in the ratio by the same number. So, for example,

$$5 : 3 \text{ is equivalent to } 15 : 9$$

and

$$\frac{3}{4} : 2 \text{ is equivalent to } 3 : 8$$

4.14   Divide a mass of 380 kg in the ratio $\frac{3}{4} : \frac{1}{5}$.

Solution   It is simpler to work with whole numbers, so first of all we produce an equivalent ratio by multiplying each term, first by 4, and then by 5, to give

$$\frac{3}{4} : \frac{1}{5} = 3 : \frac{4}{5} = 15 : 4$$

Note that this is equivalent to multiplying through by the lowest common multiple of 4 and 5.

So dividing 380 kg in the ratio $\frac{3}{4} : \frac{1}{5}$ is equivalent to dividing it in the ratio $15 : 4$.

Now the total number of parts is 19 and so we split the 380 kg mass as

$$\frac{15}{19} \times 380 = 300$$

and

$$\frac{4}{19} \times 380 = 80$$

The total mass is split into 300 kg and 80 kg.

4.15   Bell metal, which is a form of bronze, is used for casting bells. It is an alloy of copper and tin. To manufacture bell metal requires 17 parts of copper to every 3 parts of tin.

(a) Express this requirement as a ratio.

(b) Express the amount of tin required as a percentage of the total.

(c) If the total amount of tin in a particular casting is 150 kg, find the amount of copper.

Solution   (a) Copper and tin are needed in the ratio $17 : 3$.

(b) $\frac{3}{20}$ of the alloy is tin. Since $\frac{3}{20} = 15\%$ we find that 15% of the alloy is tin.

(c) A mass of 150 kg of tin makes up 15% of the total. So 1% of the total would have a mass of 10 kg. Copper, which makes up 85%, will have a mass of 850 kg.

Self-assessment question 4.2

1. Dividing a number in the ratio $2:3$ is the same as dividing it in the ratio $10:15$. True or false?

Exercise 4.2

MyMathLab

1. Divide 180 in the ratio $8:1:3$.

2. Divide 930 cm in the ratio $1:1:3$.

3. A 6 m length of wood is cut in the ratio $2:3:4$. Calculate the length of each piece.

4. Divide 1200 in the ratio $1:2:3:4$.

5. A sum of £2600 is divided between Alan, Bill and Claire in the ratio of $2\frac{3}{4}:1\frac{1}{2}:2\frac{1}{4}$. Calculate the amount that each receives.

6. A mass of 40 kg is divided into three portions in the ratio $3:4:8$. Calculate the mass of each portion.

7. Express the following ratios in their simplest forms:
   (a) $12:24$ (b) $3:6$ (c) $3:6:12$
   (d) $\frac{1}{3}:7$

8. A box contains two sizes of nails. The ratio of long nails to short nails is $2:7$. Calculate the number of each type if the total number of nails is 108.

Test and assignment exercises 4

1. Express as decimals
   (a) 8%   (b) 18%   (c) 65%

2. Express as percentages
   (a) $\dfrac{3}{8}$ (b) $\dfrac{79}{100}$ (c) $\dfrac{56}{118}$

3. Calculate 27.3% of 1496.

4. Calculate 125% of 125.

5. Calculate 85% of 0.25.

6. Divide 0.5 in the ratio $2:4:9$.

7. A bill totals £234.5 to which is added tax at 17.5%. Calculate the amount of tax to be paid.

8. An inheritance is divided between three people in the ratio $4:7:2$. If the least amount received is £2300 calculate how much the other two people received.

9. Divide 70 in the ratio of $0.5:1.3:2.1$.

10. Divide 50% in the ratio $2:3$.

11. The temperature of a liquid is reduced from 39 °C to 35 °C. Calculate the percentage change in temperature.

12. A jacket priced at £120 is reduced by 30% in a sale. Calculate the sale price of the jacket.

13. The price of a car is reduced from £7250 to £6450. Calculate the percentage change in price.

14. The population of a small town increases from 17296 to 19437 over a five-year period. Calculate the percentage change in population.

15. A number, X, is increased by 20% to form a new number Y. Y is then decreased by 20% to form a third number Z. Express Z in terms of X.

Algebra

5

This chapter:

- explains what is meant by 'algebra'
- introduces important algebraic notations
- explains what is meant by a 'power' or 'index'
- illustrates how to evaluate an expression
- explains what is meant by a 'formula'

5.1 What is algebra?

In order to extend the techniques of arithmetic so that they can be more useful in applications we introduce letters or **symbols** to represent quantities of interest. For example, we may choose the capital letter I to stand for the *interest rate* in a business calculation, or the lower case letter t to stand for the *time* in a scientific calculation, and so on. The choice of which letter to use for which quantity is largely up to the user, although some conventions have been developed. Very often the letters x and y are used to stand for arbitrary quantities. **Algebra** is the body of mathematical knowledge that has been developed to manipulate symbols. Some symbols take fixed and unchanging values, and these are known as **constants**. For example, suppose we let the symbol b stand for the boiling point of water. This is fixed at $100\,°C$ and so b is a constant. Some symbols represent quantities that can vary, and these are called **variables**. For example, the velocity of a car might be represented by the symbol v, and might vary from 0 to 100 kilometres per hour.

Algebraic notation

In algebraic work particular attention must be paid to the type of symbol used, so that, for example, the symbol T is quite different from the symbol t.

Table 5.1
The Greek alphabet

A	α	alpha	I	ι	iota	P	ρ	rho
B	β	beta	K	κ	kappa	Σ	σ	sigma
Γ	γ	gamma	Λ	λ	lambda	T	τ	tau
Δ	δ	delta	M	μ	mu	Y	υ	upsilon
E	ε	epsilon	N	ν	nu	Φ	ϕ	phi
Z	ζ	zeta	Ξ	ξ	xi	X	χ	chi
H	η	eta	O	o	omicron	Ψ	ψ	psi
Θ	θ	theta	Π	π	pi	Ω	ω	omega

Your scientific calculator is pre-programmed with the value of π. Check that you can use it.

Usually the symbols chosen are letters from the English alphabet although we frequently meet Greek letters. You may already be aware that the Greek letter 'pi', which has the symbol π, is used in the formula for the area of a circle, and is equal to the constant $3.14159\ldots$. In many calculations π can be approximated by $\frac{22}{7}$. For reference the full Greek alphabet is given in Table 5.1.

Another important feature is the position of a symbol in relation to other symbols. As we shall see in this chapter, the quantities xy, x^y, y^x and x_y all can mean quite different things. When a symbol is placed to the right and slightly higher than another symbol it is referred to as a **superscript**. So the quantity x^y contains the superscript y. Likewise, if a symbol is placed to the right and slightly lower than another symbol it is called a **subscript**. The quantity x_1 contains the subscript 1.

The arithmetic of symbols

Addition $(+)$ If the letters x and y stand for two numbers, their **sum** is written as $x + y$. Note that $x + y$ is the same as $y + x$ just as $4 + 7$ is the same as $7 + 4$.

Subtraction $(-)$ The quantity $x - y$ is called the **difference** of x and y, and means the number y subtracted from the number x. Note that $x - y$ is not the same as $y - x$, in the same way that $5 - 3$ is different from $3 - 5$.

Multiplication $(\times)$ Five times the number x is written $5 \times x$, although when multiplying the $\times$ sign is sometimes replaced with '$\cdot$', or is even left out altogether. This means that $5 \times x$, $5 \cdot x$ and $5x$ all mean five times the number x. Similarly $x \times y$ can be written $x \cdot y$ or simply xy. When multiplying, the order of the symbols is not important, so that xy is the same as yx just as 5×4 is the same as 4×5. The quantity xy is also known as the **product** of x and y.

Division $(\div)$ $x \div y$ means the number x divided by the number y. This is also written x/y. Here the order is important and x/y is quite different from y/x. An expression involving one symbol divided by another is known as an **algebraic fraction**. The top line is called the **numerator** and the bottom line is called the **denominator**. The quantity x/y is known as the **quotient** of x and y.

A quantity made up of symbols together with $+$, $-$, $\times$ or $\div$ is called an **algebraic expression**. When evaluating an algebraic expression the BODMAS rule given in Chapter 1 applies. This rule reminds us of the correct order in which to evaluate an expression.

Self-assessment questions 5.1

1. Explain what you understand by the term 'algebra'.

2. If m and n are two numbers, explain what is meant by mn.

3. What is an algebraic fraction? Explain the meaning of the terms 'numerator' and 'denominator'.

4. What is the distinction between a superscript and a subscript?

5. What is the distinction between a variable and a constant?

5.2   Powers or indices

Frequently we shall need to multiply a number by itself several times, for example $3 \times 3 \times 3$, or $a \times a \times a \times a$.

To abbreviate such quantities a new notation is introduced. $a \times a \times a$ is written a^3, pronounced 'a cubed'. The superscript 3 is called a **power** or **index** and the letter a is called the **base**. Similarly $a \times a$ is written a^2, pronounced 'a squared' or 'a raised to the power 2'.

The calculator button x^y is used to find powers of numbers.

Most calculators have a button marked x^y, which can be used to evaluate expressions such as 2^8, 3^{11} and so on. Check to see whether your calculator can do these by verifying that $2^8 = 256$ and $3^{11} = 177147$. Note that the plural of index is **indices**.

As a^2 means $a \times a$, and a^3 means $a \times a \times a$, then we interpret a^1 as simply a. That is, any number raised to the power 1 is itself.

Key point   Any number raised to the power 1 is itself, that is $a^1 = a$.

WORKED EXAMPLES

5.1   In the expression 3^8 identify the index and the base.

Solution	In the expression 3^8, the index is 8 and the base is 3.
5.2	Explain what is meant by y^5.
Solution	y^5 means $y \times y \times y \times y \times y$.
5.3	Explain what is meant by $x^2 y^3$.
Solution	x^2 means $x \times x$; y^3 means $y \times y \times y$. Therefore $x^2 y^3$ means $x \times x \times y \times y \times y$.
5.4	Evaluate 2^3 and 3^4.
Solution	2^3 means $2 \times 2 \times 2$, that is 8. Similarly 3^4 means $3 \times 3 \times 3 \times 3$, that is 81.
5.5	Explain what is meant by 7^1.
Solution	Any number to the power 1 is itself, that is 7^1 is simply 7.
5.6	Evaluate 10^2 and 10^3.
Solution	10^2 means 10×10 or 100. Similarly 10^3 means $10 \times 10 \times 10$ or 1000.
5.7	Use indices to write the expression $a \times a \times b \times b \times b$ more compactly.
Solution	$a \times a$ can be written a^2; $b \times b \times b$ can be written b^3. Therefore $a \times a \times b \times b \times b$ can be written as $a^2 \times b^3$ or simply $a^2 b^3$.
5.8	Write out fully $z^3 y^2$.
Solution	$z^3 y^2$ means $z \times z \times z \times y \times y$. Note that we could also write this as $zzzyy$.

We now consider how to deal with expressions involving not only powers but other operations as well. Recall from §5.1 that the BODMAS rule tells us the order in which operations should be carried out, but the rule makes no reference to powers. In fact, powers should be given higher priority than any other operation and evaluated first. Consider the expression -4^2. Because the power must be evaluated first -4^2 is equal to -16. On the other hand $(-4)^2$ means $(-4) \times (-4)$ which is equal to $+16$.

WORKED EXAMPLES

5.9	Simplify (a) -5^2, (b) $(-5)^2$.
Solution	(a) The power is evaluated first. Noting that $5^2 = 25$, we see that $-5^2 = -25$.
Recall that when a negative number is multiplied by another negative number the result is positive.	(b) $(-5)^2$ means $(-5) \times (-5) = +25$.
	Note how the brackets can significantly change the meaning of an expression.
5.10	Explain the meanings of $-x^2$ and $(-x)^2$. Are these different?

Solution   In the expression $-x^2$ it is the quantity x that is squared, so that $-x^2 = -(x \times x)$. On the other hand $(-x)^2$ means $(-x) \times (-x)$, which equals $+x^2$. The two expressions are not the same.

Following the previous two examples we emphasise again the importance of the position of brackets in an expression.

Self-assessment questions 5.2

1. Explain the meaning of the terms 'power' and 'base'.

2. What is meant by an index?

3. Explain the distinction between $(xyz)^2$ and xyz^2.

4. Explain the distinction between $(-3)^4$ and -3^4.

Exercise 5.2

MyMathLab

1. Evaluate the following without using a calculator: 2^4, $(\frac{1}{2})^2$, 1^8, 3^5 and 0^3.

2. Evaluate 10^4, 10^5 and 10^6 without using a calculator.

3. Use a calculator to evaluate 11^4, 16^8, 39^4 and 1.5^7.

4. Write out fully (a) a^4b^2c and (b) xy^2z^4.

5. Write the following expressions compactly using indices:
   (a) $xxxyyx$ (b) $xxyyzzz$
   (c) $xyzxyz$ (d) $abccba$

6. Using a calculator, evaluate
   (a) 7^4 (b) 7^5 (c) $7^4 \times 7^5$ (d) 7^9
   (e) 8^3 (f) 8^7 (g) $8^3 \times 8^7$ (h) 8^{10}

   Can you spot a rule for multiplying numbers with powers?

7. Without using a calculator, find $(-3)^3$, $(-2)^2$, $(-1)^7$ and $(-1)^4$.

8. Use a calculator to find $(-16.5)^3$, $(-18)^2$ and $(-0.5)^5$.

9. Without using a calculator find
   (a) $(-6)^2$ (b) $(-3)^2$ (c) $(-4)^3$
   (d) $(-2)^3$
   Carefully compare your answers with the results of finding -6^2, -3^2, -4^3 and -2^3.

5.3 Substitution and formulae

Substitution means replacing letters by actual numerical values.

WORKED EXAMPLES

5.11   Find the value of a^4 when $a = 3$.

Solution a^4 means $a \times a \times a \times a$. When we **substitute** the number 3 in place of the letter a we find 3^4 or $3 \times 3 \times 3 \times 3$, that is 81.

5.12   Find the value of $a + 7b + 3c$ when $a = 1$, $b = 2$ and $c = 3$.

Solution   Letting $b = 2$ we note that $7b = 14$. Letting $c = 3$ we note that $3c = 9$. Therefore, with $a = 1$,

$$a + 7b + 3c = 1 + 14 + 9 = 24$$

5.13   If $x = 4$, find the value of (a) $8x^3$ and (b) $(8x)^3$.

Solution   (a) Substituting $x = 4$ into $8x^3$ we find $8 \times 4^3 = 8 \times 64 = 512$.

(b) Substituting $x = 4$ into $(8x)^3$ we obtain $(32)^3 = 32768$. Note that the use of brackets makes a significant difference to the result.

5.14   Evaluate mk, mn and nk when $m = 5$, $n = -4$ and $k = 3$.

Solution $mk = 5 \times 3 = 15$. Similarly $mn = 5 \times (-4) = -20$ and $nk = (-4) \times 3 = -12$.

5.15   Find the value of $-7x$ when (a) $x = 2$ and (b) $x = -2$.

Solution   (a) Substituting $x = 2$ into $-7x$ we find -7×2, which equals -14.

(b) Substituting $x = -2$ into $-7x$ we find -7×-2, which equals 14.

5.16   Find the value of x^2 when $x = -3$.

Solution   Because x^2 means $x \times x$, its value when $x = -3$ is -3×-3, that is $+9$.

5.17   Find the value of $-x^2$ when $x = -3$.

Solution   Recall that a power is evaluated first. So $-x^2$ means $-(x \times x)$. When $x = -3$, this evaluates to $-(-3 \times -3) = -9$.

5.18   Find the value of $x^2 + 3x$ when (a) $x = 2$, (b) $x = -2$.

Solution   (a) Letting $x = 2$ we find

$$x^2 + 3x = (2)^2 + 3(2) = 4 + 6 = 10$$

(b) Letting $x = -2$ we find

$$x^2 + 3x = (-2)^2 + 3(-2) = 4 - 6 = -2$$

5.19   Find the value of $\frac{3x^2}{4} + 5x$ when $x = 2$.

Solution Letting $x = 2$ we find

$$\frac{3x^2}{4} + 5x = \frac{3(2)^2}{4} + 5(2)$$

$$= \frac{12}{4} + 10$$

$$= 13$$

5.20 Find the value of $\frac{x^3}{4}$ when $x = 0.5$.

Solution When $x = 0.5$ we find

$$\frac{x^3}{4} = \frac{0.5^3}{4} = 0.03125$$

A **formula** is used to relate two or more quantities. You may already be familiar with the common formula used to find the area of a rectangle:

area $=$ length $\times$ breadth

In symbols, writing A for area, l for length and b for breadth we have

$A = l \times b$ or simply $A = lb$

If we are now given particular numerical values for l and b we can use this formula to find A.

WORKED EXAMPLES

5.21 Use the formula $A = lb$ to find A when $l = 10$ and $b = 2.5$.

Solution Substituting the values $l = 10$ and $b = 2.5$ into the formula $A = lb$ we find $A = 10 \times 2.5 = 25$.

5.22 The formula $V = IR$ is used by electrical engineers. Find the value of V when $I = 12$ and $R = 7$.

Solution Substituting $I = 12$ and $R = 7$ in $V = IR$ we find $V = 12 \times 7 = 84$.

5.23 Use the formula $y = x^2 + 3x + 4$ to find y when $x = -2$.

Solution Substituting $x = -2$ into the formula gives

$$y = (-2)^2 + 3(-2) + 4 = 4 - 6 + 4 = 2$$

Self-assessment question 5.3

1. What is the distinction between an algebraic expression and a formula?

Exercise 5.3

1. Evaluate $3x^2y$ when $x = 2$ and $y = 5$.

2. Evaluate $8x + 17y - 2z$ when $x = 6$, $y = 1$ and $z = -2$.

3. The area A of a circle is found from the formula $A = \pi r^2$, where r is the length of the radius. Taking π to be 3.142 find the areas of the circles whose radii, in centimetres, are (a) $r = 10$, (b) $r = 3$, (c) $r = 0.2$.

4. Evaluate $3x^2$ and $(3x)^2$ when $x = 4$.

5. Evaluate $5x^2$ and $(5x)^2$ when $x = -2$.

6. If $y = 4.85$ find
   (a) $7y$ (b) y^2 (c) $5y + 2.5$
   (d) $y^3 - y$

7. If $a = 12.8$, $b = 3.6$ and $c = 9.1$ find
   (a) $a + b + c$ (b) ab (c) bc (d) abc

8. If $C = \frac{5}{9}(F - 32)$, find C when $F = 100$.

9. Evaluate (a) x^2, (b) $-x^2$ and (c) $(-x)^2$, when $x = 7$.

10. Evaluate the following when $x = -2$:
    (a) x^2 (b) $(-x)^2$ (c) $-x^2$
    (d) $3x^2$ (e) $-3x^2$ (f) $(-3x)^2$

11. Evaluate the following when $x = -3$:
    (a) $\frac{x^2}{3}$ (b) $(-x)^2$ (c) $-(\frac{x}{3})^2$
    (d) $4x^2$ (e) $-4x^2$ (f) $(-4x)^2$

12. Evaluate $x^2 - 7x + 2$ when $x = -9$.

13. Evaluate $2x^2 + 3x - 11$ when $x = -3$.

14. Evaluate $-x^2 + 3x - 5$ when $x = -1$.

15. Evaluate $-9x^2 + 2x$ when $x = 0$.

16. Evaluate $5x^2 + x + 1$ when (a) $x = 3$, (b) $x = -3$, (c) $x = 0$, (d) $x = -1$.

17. Evaluate $\frac{2x^2}{3} - \frac{x}{2}$ when
    (a) $x = 6$ (b) $x = -6$ (c) $x = 0$
    (d) $x = 1$

18. Evaluate $\frac{4x^2}{5} + 3$ when
    (a) $x = 0$ (b) $x = 1$ (c) $x = 5$
    (d) $x = -5$

19. Evaluate $\frac{x^3}{2}$ when
    (a) $x = -1$ (b) $x = 2$ (c) $x = 4$

20. Use the formula $y = \frac{x^3}{2} + 3x^2$ to find y when
    (a) $x = 0$ (b) $x = 2$ (c) $x = 3$
    (d) $x = -1$

21. If $g = 2t^2 - 1$, find g when
    (a) $t = 3$ (b) $t = 0.5$ (c) $t = -2$

22. In business calculations, the simple interest earned on an investment, I, is calculated from the formula $I = Prn$, where P is the amount invested, r is the interest rate and n is the number of time periods. Evaluate I when
    (a) $P = 15000$, $r = 0.08$ and $n = 5$
    (b) $P = 12500$, $r = 0.075$ and $n = 3$.

23. An investment earning 'compound interest' has a value, S, given by $S = P(1 + r)^n$, where P is the amount invested, r is the interest rate and n is the number of time periods. Calculate S when
    (a) $P = 8250$, $r = 0.05$ and $n = 15$
    (b) $P = 125000$, $r = 0.075$ and $n = 11$.

VIDEO

1. Using a calculator, evaluate 44^3, 0.44^2 and 32.5^3.

2. Write the following compactly using indices:

    (a) $xxxyyyy$ (b) $\dfrac{xxx}{yyyy}$ (c) a^2baab

3. Evaluate the expression $4x^3yz^2$ when $x = 2$, $y = 5$ and $z = 3$.

4. The circumference C of a circle that has a radius of length r is given by the formula $C = 2\pi r$. Find the circumference of the circle with radius 0.5 cm. Take $\pi = 3.142$.

5. Find (a) $21^2 - 16^2$, (b) $(21 - 16)^2$. Comment upon the result.

6. If $x = 4$ and $y = -3$, evaluate

    (a) xy (b) $\dfrac{x}{y}$ (c) $\dfrac{x^2}{y^2}$ (d) $\left(\dfrac{x}{y}\right)^2$

7. Evaluate $2x(x + 4)$ when $x = 7$.

8. Evaluate $4x^2 + 7x$ when $x = 9$.

9. Evaluate $3x^2 - 7x + 12$ when $x = -2$.

10. Evaluate $-x^2 - 11x + 1$ when $x = -3$.

11. The formula $I = V/R$ is used by engineers. Find I when $V = 10$ and $R = 0.01$.

12. Given the formula $A = 1/x$, find A when (a) $x = 1$, (b) $x = 2$, (c) $x = 3$.

13. From the formula $y = 1/(x^2 + x)$ find y when (a) $x = 1$, (b) $x = -1$, (c) $x = 3$.

14. Find the value of $(-1)^n$ (a) when n is an even natural number and (b) when n is an odd natural number. (A natural number is a positive whole number.)

15. Find the value of $(-1)^{n+1}$ (a) when n is an even natural number and (b) when n is an odd natural number.

Indices

6

Objectives: This chapter:

- states three laws used for manipulating indices
- shows how expressions involving indices can be simplified using the three laws
- explains the use of negative powers
- explains square roots, cube roots and fractional powers
- revises multiplication and division by powers of 10
- explains 'scientific notation' for representing very large and very small numbers

6.1 The laws of indices

Recall from Chapter 5 that an index is simply a power and that the plural of index is indices. Expressions involving indices can often be simplified if use is made of the **laws of indices**.

The first law

$$a^m \times a^n = a^{m+n}$$

In words, this states that if two numbers involving the same base but possibly different indices are to be multiplied together, their indices are added. Note that this law can be applied only if both bases are the same.

Key point   The first law: $a^m \times a^n = a^{m+n}$.

WORKED EXAMPLES

6.1   Use the first law of indices to simplify $a^4 \times a^3$.

Solution   Using the first law we have $a^4 \times a^3 = a^{4+3} = a^7$. Note that the same result could be obtained by actually writing out all the terms:

$$a^4 \times a^3 = (a \times a \times a \times a) \times (a \times a \times a) = a^7$$

6.2   Use the first law of indices to simplify $3^4 \times 3^5$.

Solution   From the first law $3^4 \times 3^5 = 3^{4+5} = 3^9$.

6.3   Simplify $a^4 a^7 b^2 b^4$.

Solution $a^4 a^7 b^2 b^4 = a^{4+7} b^{2+4} = a^{11} b^6$. Note that only those quantities with the same base can be combined using the first law.

The second law

$$\frac{a^m}{a^n} = a^{m-n}$$

In words, this states that if two numbers involving the same base but possibly different indices are to be divided, their indices are subtracted.

Key point   The second law: $\dfrac{a^m}{a^n} = a^{m-n}$.

WORKED EXAMPLES

6.4   Use the second law of indices to simplify $\frac{a^5}{a^3}$.

Solution   The second law states that we subtract the indices, that is

$$\frac{a^5}{a^3} = a^{5-3} = a^2$$

6.5   Use the second law of indices to simplify $\frac{3^7}{3^4}$.

Solution   From the second law, $\frac{3^7}{3^4} = 3^{7-4} = 3^3$.

6.6   Using the second law of indices, simplify $\frac{x^3}{x^3}$.

Solution   Using the second law of indices we have $\frac{x^3}{x^3} = x^{3-3} = x^0$. However, note that any expression divided by itself equals 1, and so $\frac{x^3}{x^3}$ must equal 1. We can conclude from this that any number raised to the power 0 equals 1.

Key point   Any number raised to the power 0 equals 1, that is $a^0 = 1$.

WORKED EXAMPLE

6.7   Evaluate (a) 14^0, (b) 0.5^0.

Solution   (a) Any number to the power 0 equals 1 and so $14^0 = 1$.

(b) Similarly, $0.5^0 = 1$.

The third law

$$(a^m)^n = a^{mn}$$

If a number is raised to a power, and the result is itself raised to a power, then the two powers are multiplied together.

Key point   The third law: $(a^m)^n = a^{mn}$.

WORKED EXAMPLES

6.8   Simplify $(3^2)^4$.

Solution   The third law states that the two powers are multiplied:

$$(3^2)^4 = 3^{2 \times 4} = 3^8$$

6.9   Simplify $(x^4)^3$.

Solution   Using the third law:

$$(x^4)^3 = x^{4 \times 3} = x^{12}$$

6.10   Remove the brackets from the expression $(2a^2)^3$.

Solution $(2a^2)^3$ means $(2a^2) \times (2a^2) \times (2a^2)$. We can write this as

$$2 \times 2 \times 2 \times a^2 \times a^2 \times a^2$$

or simply $8a^6$. We could obtain the same result by noting that both terms in the brackets, that is the 2 and the a^2, must be raised to the power 3, that is

$$(2a^2)^3 = 2^3(a^2)^3 = 8a^6$$

The result of the previous example can be generalised to any term of the form $(a^m b^n)^k$. To simplify such an expression we make use of the formula $(a^m b^n)^k = a^{mk} b^{nk}$.

Key point $(a^m b^n)^k = a^{mk} b^{nk}$

WORKED EXAMPLE

6.11   Remove the brackets from the expression $(x^2 y^3)^4$.

Solution   Using the previous result we find

$$(x^2y^3)^4 = x^8y^{12}$$

We often need to use several laws of indices in one example.

WORKED EXAMPLES

6.12   Simplify $\frac{(x^3)^4}{x^2}$.

Solution $(x^3)^4 = x^{12}$ using the third law of indices

So

$$\frac{(x^3)^4}{x^2} = \frac{x^{12}}{x^2} = x^{10}$$ using the second law

6.13   Simplify $(t^4)^2(t^2)^3$.

Solution $(t^4)^2 = t^8$, $(t^2)^3 = t^6$ using the third law

So

$$(t^4)^2(t^2)^3 = t^8t^6 = t^{14}$$ using the first law

Self-assessment questions 6.1

1. State the three laws of indices.

2. Explain what is meant by a^0.

3. Explain what is meant by x^1.

Exercise 6.1

1. Simplify
   (a) $5^7 \times 5^{13}$ (b) $9^8 \times 9^5$
   (c) $11^2 \times 11^3 \times 11^4$

2. Simplify
   (a) $\dfrac{15^3}{15^2}$ (b) $\dfrac{4^{18}}{4^9}$ (c) $\dfrac{5^{20}}{5^{19}}$

3. Simplify
   (a) a^7a^3 (b) a^4a^5 (c) $b^{11}b^{10}b$

4. Simplify
   (a) $x^7 \times x^8$ (b) $y^4 \times y^8 \times y^9$

5. Explain why the laws of indices cannot be used to simplify $19^8 \times 17^8$.

6. Simplify
    (a) $(7^3)^2$ (b) $(4^2)^8$ (c) $(7^9)^2$

7. Simplify $\dfrac{1}{(5^3)^8}$.

8. Simplify
    (a) $(x^2y^3)(x^3y^2)$ (b) $(a^2bc^2)(b^2ca)$

9. Remove the brackets from
    (a) $(x^2y^4)^5$ (b) $(9x^3)^2$ (c) $(-3x)^3$
    (d) $(-x^2y^3)^4$

10. Simplify
    (a) $\dfrac{(z^2)^3}{z^3}$ (b) $\dfrac{(y^3)^2}{(y^2)^2}$ (c) $\dfrac{(x^3)^2}{(x^2)^3}$

6.2 Negative powers

Sometimes a number is raised to a negative power. This is interpreted as follows:

$$a^{-m} = \frac{1}{a^m}$$

This can also be rearranged and expressed in the form

$$a^m = \frac{1}{a^{-m}}$$

Key point

$$a^{-m} = \frac{1}{a^m}, \qquad a^m = \frac{1}{a^{-m}}$$

For example,

$$3^{-2} \text{ means } \frac{1}{3^2}, \text{ that is } \frac{1}{9}$$

Similarly,

the number $\dfrac{1}{5^{-2}}$ can be written 5^2, or simply 25

To see the justification for this, note that because any number raised to the power 0 equals 1 we can write

$$\frac{1}{a^m} = \frac{a^0}{a^m}$$

Using the second law of indices to simplify the right-hand side we obtain $\frac{a^0}{a^m} = a^{0-m} = a^{-m}$ so that $\frac{1}{a^m}$ is the same as a^{-m}.

6.14 Evaluate

(a) 2^{-5} (b) $\dfrac{1}{3^{-4}}$

Solution   (a) $2^{-5} = \dfrac{1}{2^5} = \dfrac{1}{32}$ (b) $\dfrac{1}{3^{-4}} = 3^4$ or simply 81

6.15 Evaluate

(a) 10^{-1} (b) 10^{-2}

Solution   (a) 10^{-1} means $\frac{1}{10^1}$, or simply $\frac{1}{10}$. It is important to recognise that 10^{-1} is therefore the same as 0.1.

(b) 10^{-2} means $\frac{1}{10^2}$ or $\frac{1}{100}$. So 10^{-2} is therefore the same as 0.01.

6.16 Rewrite each of the following expressions using only positive powers:

(a) 7^{-3} (b) x^{-5}

Solution   (a) 7^{-3} means the same as $\frac{1}{7^3}$. The expression has now been written using a positive power.

(b) $x^{-5} = \frac{1}{x^5}$.

6.17 Rewrite each of the following expressions using only positive powers:

(a) $\dfrac{1}{x^{-9}}$ (b) $\dfrac{1}{a^{-4}}$

Solution   (a) $\dfrac{1}{x^{-9}} = x^9$ (b) $\dfrac{1}{a^{-4}} = a^4$

6.18 Rewrite each of the following using only negative powers:

(a) 6^8 (b) x^5 (c) z^a

Solution   (a) $6^8 = \dfrac{1}{6^{-8}}$ (b) $x^5 = \dfrac{1}{x^{-5}}$ (c) $z^a = \dfrac{1}{z^{-a}}$

6.19 Simplify

(a) $x^{-2}x^7$ (b) $\dfrac{x^{-3}}{x^{-5}}$

Solution   (a) To simplify $x^{-2}x^7$ we can use the first law of indices to write it as $x^{-2+7} = x^5$.

(b) To simplify $\dfrac{x^{-3}}{x^{-5}}$ we can use the second law of indices to write it as $x^{-3-(-5)} = x^{-3+5} = x^2$.

6.20 Simplify

(a) $(x^{-3})^5$ (b) $\dfrac{1}{(x^{-2})^2}$

(a) To simplify $(x^{-3})^5$ we can use the third law of indices and write it as $x^{-3 \times 5} = x^{-15}$. The answer could also be written as $\frac{1}{x^{15}}$.

(b) Note that $(x^{-2})^2 = x^{-4}$ using the third law. So $\frac{1}{(x^{-2})^2} = \frac{1}{x^{-4}}$. This could also be written as x^4.

Self-assessment question 6.2

1. Explain how the negative power in a^{-m} is interpreted.

Exercise 6.2

1. Without using a calculator express each of the following as a proper fraction:
   (a) 2^{-2} (b) 2^{-3} (c) 3^{-2} (d) 3^{-3}
   (e) 5^{-2} (f) 4^{-2} (g) 9^{-1} (h) 11^{-2}
   (i) 7^{-1}

2. Express each of the following as decimal fractions:
   (a) 10^{-1} (b) 10^{-2} (c) 10^{-6} (d) $\frac{1}{10^2}$
   (e) $\frac{1}{10^3}$ (f) $\frac{1}{10^4}$

3. Write each of the following using only a positive power:
   (a) x^{-4} (b) $\frac{1}{x^{-5}}$ (c) x^{-7} (d) y^{-2}
   (e) $\frac{1}{y^{-1}}$ (f) y^{-1} (g) y^{-2} (h) z^{-1}
   (i) $\frac{1}{z^{-1}}$

4. Simplify the following using the laws of indices and write your results using only positive powers:
   (a) $x^{-2}x^{-1}$ (b) $x^{-3}x^{-2}$ (c) x^3x^{-4}
   (d) $x^{-4}x^9$ (e) $\frac{x^{-2}}{x^{11}}$ (f) $(x^{-4})^2$
   (g) $(x^{-3})^3$ (h) $(x^2)^{-2}$

5. Simplify
   (a) $a^{13}a^{-2}$ (b) $x^{-9}x^{-7}$ (c) $x^{-21}x^2x$
   (d) $(4^{-3})^2$

6. Evaluate
   (a) 10^{-3} (b) 10^{-4} (c) 10^{-5}

7. Evaluate $4^{-8}/4^{-6}$ and $3^{-5}/3^{-8}$ without using a calculator.

6.3 Square roots, cube roots and fractional powers

Square roots

Consider the relationship between the numbers 5 and 25. We know that $5^2 = 25$ and so 25 is the square of 5. Equivalently we say that 5 is a **square root** of 25. The symbol $\sqrt[2]{}$, or simply $\sqrt{}$, is used to denote a square root and we write

$$5 = \sqrt{25}$$

We can picture this as follows:

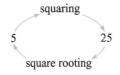

From this we see that taking the square root can be thought of as reversing the process of squaring.

We also note that

$$(-5) \times (-5) = (-5)^2$$
$$= 25$$

and so -5 is also a square root of 25. Hence we can write

$$-5 = \sqrt{25}$$

We can write both results together by using the 'plus or minus' sign $\pm$. We write

$$\sqrt{25} = \pm 5$$

In general, a **square root** of a number is a number that when squared gives the original number. Note that there are two square roots of any positive number but negative numbers possess no square roots.

Most calculators enable you to find square roots although only the positive value is normally given. Look for a $\sqrt{}$ or 'sqrt' button on your calculator.

WORKED EXAMPLE

6.21   (a)   Use your calculator to find $\sqrt{79}$ correct to 4 decimal places.

(b)   Check your answers are correct by squaring them.

Solution   (a)   Using the $\sqrt{}$ button on the calculator you should verify that

$$\sqrt{79} = 8.8882 \text{ (to 4 decimal places)}$$

The second square root is -8.8882. Thus we can write

$$\sqrt{79} = \pm 8.8882$$

(b)   Squaring either of the numbers ± 8.8882 we recover the original number, 79.

Cube roots

The **cube root** of a number is a number that when cubed gives the original number. The symbol for a cube root is $\sqrt[3]{}$. So, for example, since $2^3 = 8$ we can write $\sqrt[3]{8} = 2$.

We can picture this as follows:

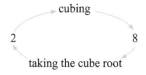

We can think of taking the cube root as reversing the process of cubing. As another example we note that $(-2)^3 = -8$ and hence $\sqrt[3]{-8} = -2$. All numbers, both positive and negative, possess a single cube root.

Your calculator may enable you to find a cube root. Look for a button marked $\sqrt[3]{}$. If so, check that you can use it correctly by verifying that

$$\sqrt[3]{46} = 3.5830$$

Fourth, fifth and other roots are defined in a similar way. For example, since

$$8^5 = 32768$$

we can write

$$\sqrt[5]{32768} = 8$$

Fractional powers

Sometimes fractional powers are used. The following example helps us to interpret a fractional power.

WORKED EXAMPLE

6.22   Simplify

(a) $x^{\frac{1}{2}}x^{\frac{1}{2}}$ (b) $x^{\frac{1}{3}}x^{\frac{1}{3}}x^{\frac{1}{3}}$

Use your results to interpret the fractional powers $\frac{1}{2}$ and $\frac{1}{3}$.

Solution   (a) Using the first law we can write

$$x^{\frac{1}{2}}x^{\frac{1}{2}} = x^{\frac{1}{2}+\frac{1}{2}} = x^1 = x$$

(b) Similarly,

$$x^{\frac{1}{3}}x^{\frac{1}{3}}x^{\frac{1}{3}} = x^{\frac{1}{3}+\frac{1}{3}+\frac{1}{3}} = x^1 = x$$

From (a) we see that

$$(x^{\frac{1}{2}})^2 = x$$

So when $x^{\frac{1}{2}}$ is squared, the result is x. Thus $x^{\frac{1}{2}}$ is simply the square root of x, that is

$$x^{\frac{1}{2}} = \sqrt{x}$$

Similarly, from (b)

$$(x^{\frac{1}{3}})^3 = x$$

and so $x^{\frac{1}{3}}$ is the cube root of x, that is

$$x^{\frac{1}{3}} = \sqrt[3]{x}$$

Key point $x^{\frac{1}{2}} = \sqrt{x}, \qquad x^{\frac{1}{3}} = \sqrt[3]{x}$

More generally we have the following result:

Key point $x^{\frac{1}{n}} = \sqrt[n]{x}$

Your scientific calculator will probably be able to find fractional powers. The button may be marked $x^{1/y}$ or $\sqrt[y]{x}$. Check that you can use it correctly by working through the following examples.

WORKED EXAMPLES

6.23   Evaluate to 3 decimal places, using a calculator:

(a) $3^{\frac{1}{4}}$ (b) $15^{1/5}$

Solution   Use your calculator to obtain the following solutions:

(a) 1.316   (b) 1.719

Note in part (a) that although the calculator gives just a single fourth root, there is another, -1.316.

6.24   Evaluate $(81)^{1/2}$.

Solution $(81)^{1/2} = \sqrt{81} = \pm 9$.

6.25   Explain what is meant by the number $27^{1/3}$.

Solution $27^{1/3}$ can be written $\sqrt[3]{27}$, that is the cube root of 27. The cube root of 27 is 3, since $3 \times 3 \times 3 = 27$, and so $27^{1/3} = 3$. Note also that since $27 = 3^3$ we can write

$(27)^{1/3} = (3^3)^{1/3} = 3^{(3 \times 1/3)}$ using the third law

$= 3^1 \quad = 3$

The following worked example shows how we deal with negative fractional powers.

6.26   Explain what is meant by the number $(81)^{-1/2}$.

Solution   Recall from our work on negative powers that $a^{-m} = 1/a^m$. Therefore we can write $(81)^{-1/2}$ as $1/(81)^{1/2}$. Now $81^{1/2} = \sqrt{81} = \pm 9$ and so

$(81)^{-1/2} = \dfrac{1}{\pm 9} = \pm \dfrac{1}{9}$

6.27   Write each of the following using a single index:

(a) $(5^2)^{\frac{1}{3}}$ (b) $(5^{-2})^{\frac{1}{3}}$

Solution   (a)   Using the third law of indices we find

$$(5^2)^{\frac{1}{3}} = 5^{2 \times \frac{1}{3}} = 5^{\frac{2}{3}}$$

Note that $(5^2)^{\frac{1}{3}}$ is the cube root of 5^2, that is $\sqrt[3]{25}$ or 2.9240.

(b)   Using the third law of indices we find

$$(5^{-2})^{\frac{1}{3}} = 5^{-2 \times \frac{1}{3}} = 5^{-\frac{2}{3}}$$

Note that there is a variety of equivalent ways in which this can be expressed, for example $\sqrt[3]{\frac{1}{5^2}}$ or $\sqrt[3]{\frac{1}{25}}$, or as $\frac{1}{5^{2/3}}$.

6.28   Write each of the following using a single index:

(a) $\sqrt{x^3}$ (b) $(\sqrt{x})^3$

Solution   (a)   Because the square root of a number can be expressed as that number raised to the power $\frac{1}{2}$ we can write

$$\sqrt{x^3} = (x^3)^{\frac{1}{2}}$$

$$= x^{3 \times \frac{1}{2}} \qquad \text{using the third law}$$

$$= x^{\frac{3}{2}}$$

(b) $(\sqrt{x})^3 = (x^{\frac{1}{2}})^3$

$$= x^{\frac{3}{2}} \qquad \text{using the third law}$$

Note from this example that $\sqrt{x^3} = (\sqrt{x})^3$.

Note that by generalising the results of the two previous worked examples we have the following:

Key point $a^{\frac{m}{n}} = \sqrt[n]{a^m} = (\sqrt[n]{a})^m$

Self-assessment questions 6.3

1. Explain the meaning of the fractional powers $x^{1/2}$ and $x^{1/3}$.

2. What are the square roots of 100? Explain why the number -100 does not have any square roots.

Exercise 6.3

1. Evaluate
   (a) $64^{1/3}$ (b) $144^{1/2}$ (c) $16^{-1/4}$

   (d) $25^{-1/2}$ (e) $\dfrac{1}{32^{-1/5}}$

2. Simplify and then evaluate
   (a) $(3^{-1/2})^4$ (b) $(8^{1/3})^{-1}$

3. Write each of the following using a single index:
   (a) $\sqrt{8}$ (b) $\sqrt[3]{12}$ (c) $\sqrt[4]{16}$ (d) $\sqrt{13^3}$
   (e) $\sqrt[3]{4^7}$

4. Write each of the following using a single index:
   (a) $\sqrt{x}$ (b) $\sqrt[3]{y}$ (c) $\sqrt[2]{x^5}$ (d) $\sqrt[3]{5^7}$

6.4 Multiplication and division by powers of 10

To multiply and divide decimal fractions by powers of 10 is particularly simple. For example, to multiply 256.875 by 10 the decimal point is moved one place to the right, that is

$$256.875 \times 10 = 2568.75$$

To multiply by 100 the decimal point is moved two places to the right. So

$$256.875 \times 100 = 25687.5$$

To divide a number by 10, the decimal point is moved one place to the left. This is equivalent to multiplying by 10^{-1}. To divide by 100, the decimal point is moved two places to the left. This is equivalent to multiplying by 10^{-2}.

   In general, to multiply a number by 10^n, the decimal point is moved n places to the right if n is a positive integer, and n places to the left if n is a negative integer. If necessary, additional zeros are inserted to make up the required number of digits. Consider the following example.

WORKED EXAMPLE

6.29 Without the use of a calculator, write down

   (a) 75.45×10^3 (b) 0.056×10^{-2} (c) 96.3×10^{-3} (d) 0.00743×10^5

Solution (a) The decimal point is moved three places to the right: $75.45 \times 10^3 = 75450$. It has been necessary to include an additional zero to make up the required number of digits.

   (b) The decimal point is moved two places to the left: $0.056 \times 10^{-2} = 0.00056$.

   (c) $96.3 \times 10^{-3} = 0.0963$.

   (d) $0.00743 \times 10^5 = 743$.

Exercise 6.4

1. Without the use of a calculator write down:
    (a) 7.43×10^2 (b) 7.43×10^4 (c) 0.007×10^4 (d) 0.07×10^{-2}

2. Write each of the following as a multiple of 10^2:
    (a) 300 (b) 356 (c) 32 (d) 0.57

6.5 Scientific notation

It is often necessary to use very large numbers such as 65000000000 or very small numbers such as 0.000000001. **Scientific notation** can be used to express such numbers in a more concise form, which avoids writing very lengthy strings of numbers. Each number is written in the form

$$a \times 10^n$$

where a is usually a number between 1 and 10. We also make use of the fact that

$$10 = 10^1, \qquad 100 = 10^2, \qquad 1000 = 10^3 \text{ and so on}$$

and also that

$$10^{-1} = \frac{1}{10} = 0.1, \qquad 10^{-2} = \frac{1}{100} = 0.01 \text{ and so on}$$

Then, for example,

the number 4000 can be written $4 \times 1000 = 4 \times 10^3$

Similarly

the number 68000 can be written $6.8 \times 10000 = 6.8 \times 10^4$

and

the number 0.09 can be written $9 \times 0.01 = 9 \times 10^{-2}$

Note that all three numbers have been written in the form $a \times 10^n$ where a lies between 1 and 10.

WORKED EXAMPLES

6.30 Express the following numbers in scientific notation:

(a) 54 (b) −276 (c) 0.3

Solution   (a) 54 can be written as 5.4×10, so in scientific notation we have 5.4×10^1.

(b) Negative numbers cause no problem: $-276 = -2.76 \times 10^2$.

(c) We can write 0.3 as 3×0.1 or 3×10^{-1}.

6.31 Write out fully the following numbers:

(a) 2.7×10^{-1} (b) 9.6×10^5 (c) -8.2×10^2

Solution   (a) $2.7 \times 10^{-1} = 0.27$.

(b) $9.6 \times 10^5 = 9.6 \times 100000 = 960000$.

(c) $-8.2 \times 10^2 = -8.2 \times 100 = -820$.

6.32 Simplify the expression $(3 \times 10^2) \times (5 \times 10^3)$.

Solution   The order in which the numbers are written down does not matter, and so we can write

$$(3 \times 10^2) \times (5 \times 10^3) = 3 \times 5 \times 10^2 \times 10^3 = 15 \times 10^5$$

Noting that $15 = 1.5 \times 10$ we can express the final answer in scientific notation:

$$15 \times 10^5 = 1.5 \times 10 \times 10^5 = 1.5 \times 10^6$$

Hence

$$(3 \times 10^2) \times (5 \times 10^3) = 1.5 \times 10^6$$

Self-assessment question 6.5

1. What is the purpose of using scientific notation?

Exercise 6.5

1. Express each of the following numbers in scientific notation:
    (a) 45   (b) 45000   (c) −450   (d) 90000000   (e) 0.15   (f) 0.00036   (g) 3.5
    (h) −13.2   (i) 1000000   (j) 0.0975   (k) 45.34

2. Write out fully the following numbers:
    (a) 3.75×10^2 (b) 3.97×10^1 (c) 1.875×10^{-1} (d) -8.75×10^{-3}

3. Simplify each of the following expressions, writing your final answer in scientific notation:
    (a) $(4 \times 10^3) \times (6 \times 10^4)$ (b) $(9.6 \times 10^4) \times (8.3 \times 10^3)$ (c) $(1.2 \times 10^{-3}) \times (8.7 \times 10^{-2})$
    (d) $\dfrac{9.37 \times 10^4}{6.14 \times 10^5}$ (e) $\dfrac{4.96 \times 10^{-2}}{9.37 \times 10^{-5}}$

1. Simplify

   (a) $\dfrac{z^5}{z^{-5}}$ (b) z^0 (c) $\dfrac{z^8 z^6}{z^{14}}$

2. Evaluate
   (a) $0.25^{1/2}$ (b) $(4096)^{1/3}$ (c) $(2601)^{1/2}$ (d) $16^{-1/2}$

3. Simplify $\dfrac{x^8 x^{-3}}{x^{-5} x^2}$.

4. Find the value of $(1/7)^0$.

5. Remove the brackets from
   (a) $(abc^2)^2$ (b) $(xy^2 z^3)^2$ (c) $(8x^2)^{-3}$

6. Express each of the following numbers in scientific notation:
   (a) 5792   (b) 98.4   (c) 0.001   (d) -66.667

Simplifying algebraic expressions

Objectives: This chapter:

- describes a number of ways in which complicated algebraic expressions can be simplified

7.1 Addition and subtraction of like terms

Like terms are multiples of the same quantity. For example, $3y$, $72y$ and $0.5y$ are all multiples of y and so are like terms. Similarly, $5x^2$, $-3x^2$ and $\frac{1}{2}x^2$ are all multiples of x^2 and so are like terms. xy, $17xy$ and $-91xy$ are all multiples of xy and are therefore like terms. Like terms can be collected together and added or subtracted in order to simplify them.

WORKED EXAMPLES

7.1 Simplify $3x + 7x - 2x$.

Solution   All three terms are multiples of x and so are like terms. Therefore $3x + 7x - 2x = 8x$.

7.2 Simplify $3x + 2y$.

Solution $3x$ and $2y$ are not like terms. One is a multiple of x and the other is a multiple of y. The expression $3x + 2y$ cannot be simplified.

7.3 Simplify $x + 7x + x^2$.

Solution   The like terms are x and $7x$. These can be simplified to $8x$. Then $x + 7x + x^2 = 8x + x^2$. Note that $8x$ and x^2 are not like terms and so this expression cannot be simplified further.

7.4 Simplify $ab + a^2 - 7b^2 + 9ab + 8b^2$.

Solution   The terms ab and $9ab$ are like terms. Similarly the terms $-7b^2$ and $8b^2$ are like terms. These can be collected together and then added or subtracted as appropriate. Thus

$$ab + a^2 - 7b^2 + 9ab + 8b^2 = ab + 9ab + a^2 - 7b^2 + 8b^2$$
$$= 10ab + a^2 + b^2$$

Exercise 7.1

MyMathLab

1. Simplify, if possible,
   (a) $5p - 10p + 11q + 8q$ (b) $-7r - 13s + 2r + z$ (c) $181z + 13r - 2$
   (d) $x^2 + 3y^2 - 2y + 7x^2$ (e) $4x^2 - 3x + 2x + 9$

2. Simplify
   (a) $5y + 8p - 17y + 9q$ (b) $7x^2 - 11x^3 + 14x^2 + y^3$ (c) $4xy + 3xy + y^2$
   (d) $xy + yx$ (e) $xy - yx$

7.2 Multiplying algebraic expressions and removing brackets

Recall that when multiplying two numbers together the order in which we write them is irrelevant. For example, both 5×4 and 4×5 equal 20.

When multiplying three or more numbers together the order in which we carry out the multiplication is also irrelevant. By this we mean, for example, that when asked to multiply $3 \times 4 \times 5$ we can think of this as either $(3 \times 4) \times 5$ or as $3 \times (4 \times 5)$. Check for yourself that the result is the same, 60, either way.

It is also important to appreciate that $3 \times 4 \times 5$ could have been written as $(3)(4)(5)$.

It is essential that you grasp these simple facts about numbers in order to understand the algebra that follows. This is because identical rules are applied. Rules for determining the sign of the answer when multiplying positive and negative algebraic expressions are also the same as those used for multiplying numbers.

Key point   When multiplying

$$\text{positive} \times \text{positive} = \text{positive}$$
$$\text{positive} \times \text{negative} = \text{negative}$$
$$\text{negative} \times \text{positive} = \text{negative}$$
$$\text{negative} \times \text{negative} = \text{positive}$$

We introduce the processes involved in removing brackets using some simple examples.

7.5 Simplify $3(4x)$.

Solution Just as with numbers $3(4x)$ could be written as $3 \times (4 \times x)$, and then as $(3 \times 4) \times x$, which evaluates to $12x$.
So $3(4x) = 12x$.

7.6 Simplify $5(3y)$.

Solution $5(3y) = 5 \times 3 \times y = 15y$.

7.7 Simplify $(5a)(3a)$.

Solution Here we can write $(5a)(3a) = (5 \times a) \times (3 \times a)$. Neither the order in which we carry out the multiplications nor the order in which we write down the terms matters, and so we can write this as

$$(5a)(3a) = (5 \times 3)(a \times a)$$

As we have shown, it is usual to write numbers at the beginning of an expression. This simplifies to $15 \times a^2$, that is $15a^2$. Hence

$$(5a)(3a) = 15a^2$$

7.8 Simplify $4x^2 \times 7x^5$.

Solution Recall that, when multiplying, the order in which we write down the terms does not matter. Therefore we can write

$$4x^2 \times 7x^5 = 4 \times 7 \times x^2 \times x^5$$

which equals $28x^{2+5} = 28x^7$.

7.9 Simplify $7(2b^2)$.

Solution $7(2b^2) = 7 \times (2 \times b^2) = (7 \times 2) \times b^2 = 14b^2$.

7.10 Simplify $(a) \times (-b)$

Solution Here we have the product of a positive and a negative quantity. The result will be negative. We write

$$(a) \times (-b) = -ab$$

7.11 Explain the distinction between ab^2 and $(ab)^2$.

Solution ab^2 means $a \times b \times b$ whereas $(ab)^2$ means $(ab) \times (ab)$ which equals $a \times b \times a \times b$. The latter could also be written as a^2b^2.

7.12 Simplify (a) $(6z)(8z)$, (b) $(6z) + (8z)$, noting the distinction between the two results.

Solution   (a) $(6z)(8z) = 48z^2$.

(b) $(6z) + (8z)$ is the addition of like terms. This simplifies to $14z$.

7.13   Simplify (a) $(6x)(-2x)$, (b) $(-3y^2)(-2y)$.

Solution   (a) $(6x)(-2x)$ means $(6x) \times (-2x)$, which equals $-12x^2$.

(b) $(-3y^2)(-2y) = (-3y^2) \times (-2y) = 6y^3$.

Self-assessment questions 7.2

1. Two negative expressions are multiplied together. State the sign of the resulting product.

2. Three negative expressions are multiplied together. State the sign of the resulting product.

Exercise 7.2

1. Simplify each of the following:
   (a) $(4)(3)(7)$ (b) $(7)(4)(3)$ (c) $(3)(4)(7)$

2. Simplify
   (a) $5 \times (4 \times 2)$ (b) $(5 \times 4) \times 2$

3. Simplify each of the following:
   (a) $7(2z)$ (b) $15(2y)$ (c) $(2)(3)x$
   (d) $9(3a)$ (e) $(11)(5a)$ (f) $2(3x)$

4. Simplify each of the following:
   (a) $5(4x^2)$ (b) $3(2y^3)$ (c) $11(2u^2)$
   (d) $(2 \times 4) \times u^2$ (e) $(13)(2z^2)$

5. Simplify
   (a) $(7x)(3x)$ (b) $3a(7a)$ (c) $14a(a)$

6. Simplify
   (a) $5y(3y)$ (b) $5y + 3y$
   Explain why the two results are not the same.

7. Simplify the following:
   (a) $(abc)(a^2bc)$ (b) $x^2y(xy)$
   (c) $(xy^2)(xy^2)$

8. Explain the distinction, if any, between $(xy^2)(xy^2)$ and xy^2xy^2.

9. Explain the distinction, if any, between $(xy^2)(xy^2)$ and $(xy^2) + (xy^2)$.
   In both cases simplify the expressions.

10. Simplify
    (a) $(3z)(-7z)$ (b) $3z - 7z$

11. Simplify
    (a) $(-x)(3x)$ (b) $-x + 3x$

12. Simplify
    (a) $(-2x)(-x)$ (b) $-2x - x$

7.3 Removing brackets from $a(b + c)$, $a(b - c)$ and $(a + b)(c + d)$

Recall from your study of arithmetic that the expression $(5 - 4) + 7$ is different from $5 - (4 + 7)$ because of the position of the brackets. In order to simplify an expression it is often necessary to remove brackets.

Removing brackets from expressions of the form $a(b + c)$ and $a(b - c)$

In an expression such as $a(b + c)$, it is intended that the a multiplies all the bracketed terms:

Key point

$$a(b + c) = ab + ac \qquad \text{Similarly:} \quad a(b - c) = ab - ac$$

WORKED EXAMPLES

7.14   Remove the brackets from

(a) $6(x + 5)$ (b) $8(2x - 4)$

Solution   (a) In the expression $6(x + 5)$ it is intended that the 6 multiplies both terms in the brackets. Therefore

$$6(x + 5) = 6x + 30$$

(b) In the expression $8(2x - 4)$ the 8 multiplies both terms in the brackets so that

$$8(2x - 4) = 16x - 32$$

7.15   Remove the brackets from the expression $7(5x + 3y)$.

Solution   The 7 multiplies both the terms in the bracket. Therefore

$$7(5x + 3y) = 7(5x) + 7(3y) = 35x + 21y$$

7.16   Remove the brackets from $-(x + y)$.

Solution   The expression $-(x + y)$ actually means $-1(x + y)$. It is intended that the -1 multiplies both terms in the brackets, therefore

$$-(x + y) = -1(x + y) = (-1) \times x + (-1) \times y = -x - y$$

7.17   Remove the brackets from the expression

$$(x + y)z$$

Solution   Note that the order in which we write down the terms to be multiplied does not matter, so that we can write $(x + y)z$ as $z(x + y)$. Then

$$z(x + y) = zx + zy$$

Alternatively note that $(x + y)z = xz + yz$, which is an equivalent form of the answer.

7.18   Remove the brackets from the expressions

VIDEO

(a) $5(x - 2y)$ (b) $(x + 3)(-1)$

Solution   (a) $5(x - 2y) = 5x - 5(2y) = 5x - 10y$.

(b) $(x + 3)(-1) = (-1)(x + 3) = -1x - 3 = -x - 3$.

7.19   Simplify $x + 8(x - y)$.

Solution   An expression such as this is simplified by first removing the brackets and then collecting together like terms. Removing the brackets we find

$$x + 8(x - y) = x + 8x - 8y$$

Collecting like terms we obtain $9x - 8y$.

7.20   Remove the brackets from

(a) $\frac{1}{2}(x + 2)$ (b) $\frac{1}{2}(x - 2)$ (c) $-\frac{1}{3}(a + b)$

Solution   (a) In the expression $\frac{1}{2}(x + 2)$ it is intended that the $\frac{1}{2}$ multiplies both the terms in the brackets. So

$$\frac{1}{2}(x + 2) = \frac{1}{2}x + \frac{1}{2}(2) = \frac{1}{2}x + 1$$

(b) Similarly,

$$\frac{1}{2}(x - 2) = \frac{1}{2}x - \frac{1}{2}(2) = \frac{1}{2}x - 1$$

(c) In the expression $-\frac{1}{3}(a + b)$ the term $-\frac{1}{3}$ multiplies both terms in the brackets. So

$$-\frac{1}{3}(a + b) = -\frac{1}{3}a - \frac{1}{3}b$$

Removing brackets from expressions of the form $(a + b)(c + d)$

In the expression $(a + b)(c + d)$ it is intended that the quantity $(a + b)$ multiplies both the c and the d in the second brackets. Therefore

$$(a + b)(c + d) = (a + b)c \quad + \quad (a + b)d$$

Each of these two terms can be expanded further to give

$$(a + b)c = ac + bc \qquad \text{and} \qquad (a + b)d = ad + bd$$

Therefore

Key point $$(a + b)(c + d) = ac + bc + ad + bd$$

WORKED EXAMPLES

7.21   Remove the brackets from $(3 + x)(2 + y)$.

Solution $(3 + x)(2 + y) = (3 + x)(2) + (3 + x)y$

$$= 6 + 2x + 3y + xy$$

7.22   Remove the brackets from $(x + 6)(x - 3)$.

Solution $(x + 6)(x - 3) = (x + 6)x + (x + 6)(-3)$

$$= x^2 + 6x - 3x - 18$$

$$= x^2 + 3x - 18$$

7.23   Remove the brackets from

(a) $(1 - x)(2 - x)$ (b) $(-x - 2)(2x - 1)$

Solution   (a) $(1 - x)(2 - x) = (1 - x)2 + (1 - x)(-x)$

$$= 2 - 2x - x + x^2$$

$$= 2 - 3x + x^2$$

(b) $(-x - 2)(2x - 1) = (-x - 2)(2x) + (-x - 2)(-1)$

$$= -2x^2 - 4x + x + 2$$

$$= -2x^2 - 3x + 2$$

7.24   Remove the brackets from the expression $3(x + 1)(x - 1)$.

VIDEO

Solution   First consider the expression $(x + 1)(x - 1)$:

$$(x + 1)(x - 1) = (x + 1)x + (x + 1)(-1)$$

$$= x^2 + x - x - 1$$

$$= x^2 - 1$$

Then $3(x + 1)(x - 1) = 3(x^2 - 1) = 3x^2 - 3$.

Exercise 7.3   MyMathLab

1. Remove the brackets from
   (a) $4(x + 1)$ (b) $-4(x + 1)$
   (c) $4(x - 1)$ (d) $-4(x - 1)$

2. Remove the brackets from the following expressions:
   (a) $5(x - y)$ (b) $19(x + 3y)$
   (c) $8(a + b)$ (d) $(5 + x)y$
   (e) $12(x + 4)$ (f) $17(x - 9)$
   (g) $-(a - 2b)$ (h) $\frac{1}{2}(2x + 1)$
   (i) $-3m(-2 + 4m + 3n)$

3. Remove the brackets and simplify the following:
   (a) $18 - 13(x + 2)$ (b) $x(x + y)$

4. Remove the brackets and simplify the following expressions:
   (a) $(x + 1)(x + 6)$ (b) $(x + 4)(x + 5)$
   (c) $(x - 2)(x + 3)$ (d) $(x + 6)(x - 1)$
   (e) $(x + y)(m + n)$ (f) $(4 + y)(3 + x)$
   (g) $(5 - x)(5 + x)$
   (h) $(17x + 2)(3x - 5)$

5. Remove the brackets and simplify the following expressions:
   (a) $(x+3)(x-7)$ (b) $(2x-1)(3x+7)$
   (c) $(4x+1)(4x-1)$
   (d) $(x+3)(x-3)$ (e) $(2-x)(3+2x)$

6. Remove the brackets and simplify the following expressions:
   (a) $\dfrac{1}{2}(x+2y)+\dfrac{7}{2}(4x-y)$

   (b) $\dfrac{3}{4}(x-1)+\dfrac{1}{4}(2x+8)$

7. Remove the brackets from
   (a) $-(x-y)$ (b) $-(a+2b)$
   (c) $-\dfrac{1}{2}(3p+q)$

8. Remove the brackets from $(x+1)(x+2)$. Use your result to remove the brackets from $(x+1)(x+2)(x+3)$.

Test and assignment exercises 7

1. Simplify
   (a) $7x^2+4x^2+9x-8x$ (b) $y+7-18y+1$ (c) $a^2+b^2+a^3-3b^2$

2. Simplify
   (a) $(3a^2b)\times(-a^3b^2c)$ (b) $\dfrac{x^3}{-x^2}$

3. Remove the brackets from
   (a) $(a+3b)(7a-2b)$ (b) $x^2(x+2y)$ (c) $x(x+y)(x-y)$

4. Remove the brackets from
   (a) $(7x+2)(3x-1)$ (b) $(1-x)(x+3)$ (c) $(5+x)x$ (d) $(8x+4)(7x-2)$

5. Remove the brackets and simplify
   (a) $3x(x+2)-7x^2$ (b) $-(2a+3b)(a+b)$ (c) $4(x+7)+13(x-2)$
   (d) $5(2a+5)-3(5a-2)$ (e) $\dfrac{1}{2}(a+4b)+\dfrac{3}{2}a$

Functions

Objectives: This chapter:

- explains what is meant by a function
- describes the notation used to write functions
- explains the terms 'independent variable' and 'dependent variable'
- explains what is meant by a composite function
- explains what is meant by the inverse of a function

16.1 Definition of a function

A **function** is a rule that receives an input and produces an output. It is shown schematically in Figure 16.1. For example, the rule may be 'add 2 to the input'. If 6 is the input, then $6 + 2 = 8$ will be the output. If -5 is the

Figure 16.1
A function produces an output from an input

input, then $-5 + 2 = -3$ will be the output. In general, if x is the input then $x + 2$ will be the output. Figure 16.2 illustrates this function schematically.

Figure 16.2
The function adds 2 to the input

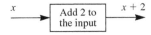

For a rule to be a function then it is crucial that only *one* output is produced for any given input.

Key point   A function is a rule that produces a *single* output for any given input.

The input to a function can usually take many values and so is called a **variable**. The output, too, varies depending upon the value of the input, and so is also a variable. The input is referred to as the **independent variable** because we are free to choose its value. The output is called the **dependent variable** because its value depends upon the value of the input.

16.2 Notation used for functions

We usually denote the input, the output and the function by letters or symbols. Commonly we use x to represent the input, y the output and f the function, although other letters will be used as well.

Consider again the example from §16.1. We let f be the function 'add 2 to the input' and we let x be the input. In mathematical notation we write

$$f : x \rightarrow x + 2$$

This means that the function f takes an input x and produces an output $x + 2$.

An alternative, but commonly used, notation is

$$f(x) = x + 2$$

The quantity $f(x)$ does not mean f times x but rather indicates that the function f acts on the quantity in the brackets. Because we also call the output y we can write $y = f(x) = x + 2$, or simply $y = x + 2$.

We could represent the same function using different letters. If h represents the function and t the input then we can write

$$h(t) = t + 2$$

WORKED EXAMPLES

16.1 A function multiplies the input by 4. Write down the function in mathematical notation.

Solution Let us call the function f and the input x. Then we have

$$f : x \rightarrow 4x \quad \text{or alternatively} \quad f(x) = 4x$$

If we call the output y, we can write $y = f(x) = 4x$, or simply $y = 4x$.

16.2 A function divides the input by 6 and then adds 3 to the result. Write the function in mathematical notation.

Solution   Let us call the function z and the input t. Then we have

$$z(t) = \frac{t}{6} + 3$$

16.3   A function f is given by the rule $f : x \rightarrow 9$, or alternatively as $f(x) = 9$. Describe in words what this function does.

Solution   Whatever the value of the input to this function, the output is always 9.

16.4   A function squares the input and then multiplies the result by 6. Write down the function using mathematical notation.

Solution   Let us call the function f, the input x and the output y. Then

$$y = f(x) = 6x^2$$

16.5   Describe in words what the following functions do:

(a) $h(x) = \dfrac{1}{x}$ (b) $g(t) = t + t^2$

Solution   (a) The function $h(x) = \dfrac{1}{x}$ divides 1 by the input.

(b) The function $g(t) = t + t^2$ adds the input to the square of the input.

Often we are given a function and need to calculate the output from a given input.

WORKED EXAMPLES

16.6   A function f is defined by $f(x) = 3x + 1$. Calculate the output when the input is (a) 4, (b) -1, (c) 0.

Solution   The function f multiplies the input by 3 and then adds 1 to the result.

(a) When the input is 4, the output is $3 \times 4 + 1 = 12 + 1 = 13$. We write

$$f(x = 4) = 3(4) + 1 = 12 + 1 = 13$$

or more simply

$$f(4) = 13$$

Note that 4 has been substituted for x in the formula for f.

(b) We require the output when the input is -1, that is $f(-1)$:

$$f(x = -1) = f(-1) = 3(-1) + 1 = -3 + 1 = -2$$

The output is -2 when the input is -1.

(c) We require the output when the input is 0, that is $f(0)$:

$$f(x = 0) = f(0) = 3(0) + 1 = 0 + 1 = 1$$

16.7 A function g is defined by $g(t) = 2t^2 - 1$. Find

(a) $g(3)$ (b) $g(0.5)$ (c) $g(-2)$

Solution (a) We obtain $g(3)$ by substituting 3 for t:

$$g(3) = 2(3)^2 - 1 = 2(9) - 1 = 17$$

(b) $g(0.5) = 2(0.5)^2 - 1 = 0.5 - 1 = -0.5$.

(c) $g(-2) = 2(-2)^2 - 1 = 8 - 1 = 7$.

16.8 A function h is defined by $h(x) = \dfrac{x}{3} + 1$. Find

(a) $h(3)$ (b) $h(t)$ (c) $h(\alpha)$ (d) $h(2\alpha)$ (e) $h(2x)$

Solution (a) If $h(x) = \dfrac{x}{3} + 1$ then $h(3) = \dfrac{3}{3} + 1 = 1 + 1 = 2$.

(b) The function h divides the input by 3 and then adds 1. We require the output when the input is t, that is we require $h(t)$. Now

$$h(t) = \frac{t}{3} + 1$$

since the input t has been divided by 3 and then 1 has been added to the result. Note that $h(t)$ is obtained by substituting t in place of x in $h(x)$.

(c) We require the output when the input is α. This is obtained by substituting α in place of x. We find

$$h(\alpha) = \frac{\alpha}{3} + 1$$

(d) We require the output when the input is 2α. We substitute 2α in place of x. This gives

$$h(2\alpha) = \frac{2\alpha}{3} + 1$$

(e) We require the output when the input is $2x$. We substitute $2x$ in place of x. That is,

$$h(2x) = \frac{2x}{3} + 1$$

16.9 Given $f(x) = x^2 + x - 1$ write expressions for

(a) $f(\alpha)$ (b) $f(x+1)$ (c) $f(2t)$

Solution (a) Substituting α in place of x we obtain

$$f(\alpha) = \alpha^2 + \alpha - 1$$

(b) Substituting $x + 1$ for x we obtain

$$f(x + 1) = (x + 1)^2 + (x + 1) - 1$$
$$= x^2 + 2x + 1 + x + 1 - 1$$
$$= x^2 + 3x + 1$$

(c) Substituting $2t$ in place of x we obtain

$$f(2t) = (2t)^2 + 2t - 1 = 4t^2 + 2t - 1$$

$<$ is the symbol for less than.
$\leqslant$ is the symbol for less than or equal to.
$\geqslant$ is the symbol for greater than or equal to.

Sometimes a function uses different rules on different intervals. For example, we could define a function as

$$f(x) = \begin{cases} 3x & \text{when} & 0 \leqslant x \leqslant 4 \\ 2x + 6 & \text{when} & 4 < x < 5 \\ 9 & \text{when} & x \geqslant 5 \end{cases}$$

Here the function is defined in three 'pieces'. The value of x determines which part of the definition is used to evaluate the function. The function is said to be a **piecewise** function.

WORKED EXAMPLE

16.10   A piecewise function is defined by

$$y(x) = \begin{cases} x^2 + 1 & \text{when} & -1 \leqslant x \leqslant 2 \\ 3x & \text{when} & 2 < x \leqslant 6 \\ 2x + 1 & \text{when} & x > 6 \end{cases}$$

Evaluate
(a) $y(0)$ (b) $y(4)$ (c) $y(2)$ (d) $y(7)$

Solution   (a) We require the value of y when $x = 0$. Since 0 lies between -1 and 2 we use the first part of the definition, that is $y = x^2 + 1$. Hence

$$y(0) = 0^2 + 1 = 1$$

(b) We require y when $x = 4$. The second part of the definition must be used because x lies between 2 and 6. Therefore

$$y(4) = 3(4) = 12$$

(c) We require y when $x = 2$. The value $x = 2$ occurs in the first part of the definition. Therefore

$$y(2) = 2^2 + 1 = 5$$

(d) We require y when $x = 7$. The final part of the function must be used. Therefore

$$y(7) = 2(7) + 1 = 15$$

Self-assessment questions 16.2

1. Explain what is meant by a function.

2. Explain the meaning of the terms 'dependent variable' and 'independent variable'.

3. Given $f(x)$, is the statement '$f(1/x)$ means $1/f(x)$' true or false?

4. Give an example of a function $f(x)$ such that $f(2) = f(3)$, that is the outputs for the inputs 2 and 3 are identical.

Exercise 16.2

MyMathLab

1. Describe in words each of the following functions:
   (a) $h(t) = 10t$ (b) $g(x) = -x + 2$
   (c) $h(t) = 3t^4$ (d) $f(x) = \dfrac{4}{x^2}$
   (e) $f(x) = 3x^2 - 2x + 9$ (f) $f(x) = 5$
   (g) $f(x) = 0$

2. Describe in words each of the following functions:
   (a) $f(t) = 3t^2 + 2t$ (b) $g(x) = 3x^2 + 2x$
   Comment upon your answers.

3. Write the following functions using mathematical notation:
   (a) The input is cubed and the result is divided by 12.
   (b) The input is added to 3 and the result is squared.
   (c) The input is squared and added to 4 times the input. Finally, 10 is subtracted from the result.
   (d) The input is squared and added to 5. Then the input is divided by this result.
   (e) The input is cubed and then 1 is subtracted from the result.

   (f) 1 is subtracted from the input and the result is squared.
   (g) Twice the input is subtracted from 7 and the result is divided by 4.
   (h) The output is always -13 whatever the value of the input.

4. Given the function $A(n) = n^2 - n + 1$ evaluate
   (a) $A(2)$ (b) $A(3)$ (c) $A(0)$
   (d) $A(-1)$

5. Given $y(x) = (2x - 1)^2$ evaluate
   (a) $y(1)$ (b) $y(-1)$ (c) $y(-3)$
   (d) $y(0.5)$ (e) $y(-0.5)$

6. The function f is given by $f(t) = 4t + 6$. Write expressions for
   (a) $f(t + 1)$ (b) $f(t + 2)$
   (c) $f(t + 1) - f(t)$ (d) $f(t + 2) - f(t)$

7. The function $f(x)$ is defined by $f(x) = 2x^2 - 3$. Write expressions for
   (a) $f(n)$ (b) $f(z)$ (c) $f(t)$ (d) $f(2t)$
   (e) $f\left(\dfrac{1}{z}\right)$ (f) $f\left(\dfrac{3}{n}\right)$ (g) $f(-x)$
   (h) $f(-4x)$ (i) $f(x + 1)$ (j) $f(2x - 1)$

8. Given the function $a(p) = p^2 + 3p + 1$ write an expression for $a(p+1)$. Verify that $a(p+1) - a(p) = 2p + 4$.

9. Sometimes the output from one function forms the input to another function. Suppose we have two functions: f given by $f(t) = 2t$, and h given by $h(t) = t + 1$. $f(h(t))$ means that t is input to h, and the output from h is input to f. Evaluate
   (a) $f(3)$ (b) $h(2)$ (c) $f(h(2))$
   (d) $h(f(3))$

10. The functions f and h are defined as in Question 9. Write down expressions for
    (a) $f(h(t))$ (b) $h(f(t))$

11. A function is defined by
$$f(x) = \begin{cases} x & 0 \leqslant x < 1 \\ 2 & x = 1 \\ 1 & x > 1 \end{cases}$$
    Evaluate
    (a) $f(0.5)$ (b) $f(1.1)$ (c) $f(1)$

16.3 Composite functions

Sometimes we wish to apply two or more functions, one after the other. The output of one function becomes the input of the next function.

Suppose $f(x) = 2x$ and $g(x) = x + 3$. We note that the function $f(x)$ doubles the input while the function $g(x)$ adds 3 to the input. Now, we let the output of $g(x)$ become the input to $f(x)$. Figure 16.3 illustrates the position.

Figure 16.3
The output of g is the input of f

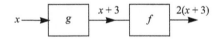

We have

$$g(x) = x + 3$$

$$f(x + 3) = 2(x + 3) = 2x + 6$$

Note that $f(x + 3)$ may be written as $f(g(x))$. Referring to Figure 16.3 we see that the initial input is x and that the final output is $2x + 6$. The functions $g(x)$ and $f(x)$ have been combined. We call $f(g(x))$ a **composite function**. It is composed of the individual functions $f(x)$ and $g(x)$. In this example we have

$$f(g(x)) = 2x + 6$$

WORKED EXAMPLES

16.11   Given $f(x) = 2x$ and $g(x) = x + 3$ find the composite function $g(f(x))$.

Solution   The output of $f(x)$ becomes the input to $g(x)$. Figure 16.4 illustrates this.

Figure 16.4
The composite function
$g(f(x))$

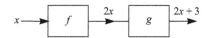

We see that

$$g(f(x)) = g(2x)$$

$$= 2x + 3$$

Note that in general $f(g(x))$ and $g(f(x))$ are different functions.

16.12   Given $f(t) = t^2 + 1$, $g(t) = \frac{3}{t}$ and $h(t) = 2t$ determine each of the following composite functions:

(a) $f(g(t))$ (b) $g(h(t))$ (c) $f(h(t))$ (d) $f(g(h(t)))$ (e) $g(f(h(t)))$

Solution   (a) $f(g(t)) = f\left(\dfrac{3}{t}\right) = \left(\dfrac{3}{t}\right)^2 + 1 = \dfrac{9}{t^2} + 1$

(b) $g(h(t)) = g(2t) = \dfrac{3}{2t}$

(c) $f(h(t)) = f(2t) = (2t)^2 + 1 = 4t^2 + 1$

(d) $f(g(h(t))) = f\left(\dfrac{3}{2t}\right)$ using (b)

$$= \left(\dfrac{3}{2t}\right)^2 + 1$$

$$= \dfrac{9}{4t^2} + 1$$

(e) $g(f(h(t))) = g(4t^2 + 1)$ using (c)

$$= \dfrac{3}{4t^2 + 1}$$

Self-assessment questions 16.3

1. Explain the term 'composite function'.

2. Give examples of functions $f(x)$ and $g(x)$ such that $f(g(x))$ and $g(f(x))$ are equal.

Exercise 16.3

MyMathLab

1. Given $f(x) = 4x$ and $g(x) = 3x - 2$ find
   (a) $f(g(x))$ (b) $g(f(x))$

2. If $x(t) = t^3$ and $y(t) = 2t$ find
   (a) $y(x(t))$ (b) $x(y(t))$

3. Given $r(x) = \dfrac{1}{2x}$, $s(x) = 3x$ and
   $t(x) = x - 2$ find
   (a) $r(s(x))$ (b) $t(s(x))$ (c) $t(r(s(x)))$
   (d) $r(t(s(x)))$ (e) $r(s(t(x)))$

4. A function can be combined with itself.
   This is known as **self-composition**. Given
   $v(t) = 2t + 1$ find
   (a) $v(v(t))$ (b) $v(v(v(t)))$

5. Given $m(t) = (t + 1)^3$, $n(t) = t^2 - 1$ and
   $p(t) = t^2$ find
   (a) $m(n(t))$ (b) $n(m(t))$ (c) $m(p(t))$
   (d) $p(m(t))$ (e) $n(p(t))$ (f) $p(n(t))$
   (g) $m(n(p(t)))$ (h) $p(p(t))$ (i) $n(n(t))$
   (j) $m(m(t))$

16.4 The inverse of a function

Note that the symbol f^{-1}
does not mean $\dfrac{1}{f}$.

We have described a function f as a rule which receives an input, say x, and generates an output, say y. We now consider the reversal of that process, namely finding a function which receives y as input and generates x as the output. If such a function exists it is called the **inverse function** of f. Figure 16.5 illustrates this schematically. The inverse of $f(x)$ is denoted by $f^{-1}(x)$.

Figure 16.5
The inverse of f reverses
the effect of f

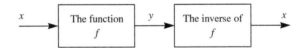

WORKED EXAMPLES

16.13   The functions f and g are defined by

$$f(x) = 2x \qquad g(x) = \frac{x}{2}$$

(a) Verify that f is the inverse of g.

(b) Verify that g is the inverse of f.

Solution   (a) The function g receives an input of x and generates an output of $x/2$; that is, it halves the input. In order to reverse the process, the inverse of g should receive $x/2$ as input and generate x as output. Now consider the function $f(x) = 2x$. This function doubles the input. Hence

$$f\left(\frac{x}{2}\right) = 2\left(\frac{x}{2}\right) = x$$

The function f has received $x/2$ as input and generated x as output. Hence f is the inverse of g. This is shown schematically in Figure 16.6.

Figure 16.6
The function f is the inverse of g

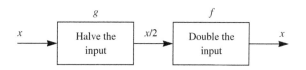

(b) The function f receives x as input and generates $2x$ as output. In order to reverse the process, the inverse of f should receive $2x$ as input and generate x as output. Now $g(x) = x/2$, that is the input is halved, and so

$$g(2x) = \frac{2x}{2} = x$$

Hence g is the inverse of f. This is shown schematically in Figure 16.7.

Figure 16.7
The function g is the inverse of f

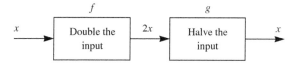

16.14   Find the inverse of the function $f(x) = 3x - 4$.

Solution   The function f multiplies the input by 3 and subtracts 4 from the result. To reverse the process, the inverse function, g say, must add 4 to the input and then divide the result by 3. Hence

$$g(x) = \frac{x + 4}{3}$$

16.15   Find the inverse of $h(t) = -\frac{1}{2}t + 5$.

Solution   The function h multiplies the input by $-\frac{1}{2}$ and then adds 5 to the result. Therefore the inverse function, g say, must subtract 5 from the input and then divide the result by $-\frac{1}{2}$. Hence

$$g(t) = \frac{(t - 5)}{-1/2} = -2(t - 5) = -2t + 10$$

There is an algebraic method of finding an inverse function that is often easier to apply. Suppose we wish to find the inverse of the function $f(x) = 6 - 2x$. We let

$$y = 6 - 2x$$

and then transpose this for x. This gives

$$x = \frac{6 - y}{2}$$

Finally, we interchange x and y to give $y = (6 - x)/2$. This is the required inverse function. To summarize these stages:

Key point   To find the inverse of $y = f(x)$,

- transpose the formula to make x the subject
- interchange x and y

The result is the required inverse function.

We shall meet some functions that do not have an inverse function. For example, consider the function $f(x) = x^2$. If 3 is the input, the output is 9. Now if -3 is the input, the output will also be 9 since $(-3)^2 = 9$. In order to reverse this process an inverse function would have to take an input of 9 and produce outputs of both 3 and -3. However, this contradicts the definition of a function, which states that a function must have only *one* output for a given input. We say that $f(x) = x^2$ does not have an inverse function.

Self-assessment questions 16.4

1. Explain what is meant by the inverse of a function.

2. Explain why the function $f(x) = 4x^4$ does not possess an inverse function.

Exercise 16.4

1. Find the inverse of each of the following functions:
   (a) $f(x) = 3x$ (b) $f(x) = \dfrac{x}{4}$
   (c) $f(x) = x + 1$ (d) $f(x) = x - 3$
   (e) $f(x) = 3 - x$ (f) $f(x) = 2x + 6$
   (g) $f(x) = 7 - 3x$ (h) $f(x) = \dfrac{1}{x}$
   (i) $f(x) = \dfrac{3}{x}$ (j) $f(x) = -\dfrac{3}{4x}$

2. Find the inverse, $f^{-1}(x)$, when $f(x)$ is given by
   (a) $6x$ (b) $6x + 1$ (c) $x + 6$
   (d) $\dfrac{x}{6}$ (e) $\dfrac{6}{x}$

3. Find the inverse, $g^{-1}(t)$, when $g(t)$ is given by

   (a) $3t + 1$ (b) $\dfrac{1}{3t + 1}$

   (c) t^3 (d) $3t^3$

   (e) $3t^3 + 1$ (f) $\dfrac{3}{t^3 + 1}$

4. The functions $g(t)$ and $h(t)$ are defined by

   $$g(t) = 2t - 1, \; h(t) = 4t + 3$$

   Find
   (a) the inverse of $h(t)$, that is $h^{-1}(t)$
   (b) the inverse of $g(t)$, that is $g^{-1}(t)$
   (c) $g^{-1}(h^{-1}(t))$ (d) $h(g(t))$
   (e) the inverse of $h(g(t))$
   What observations do you make from (c) and (e)?

Test and assignment exercises 16

1. Given $r(t) = t^2 - t/2 + 4$ evaluate

   (a) $r(0)$ (b) $r(-1)$ (c) $r(2)$ (d) $r(3.6)$ (e) $r(-4.6)$

2. A function is defined as $h(t) = t^2 - 7$.

   (a) State the dependent variable.   (b) State the independent variable.

3. Given the functions $a(x) = x^2 + 1$ and $b(x) = 2x + 1$ write expressions for

   (a) $a(\alpha)$ (b) $b(t)$ (c) $a(2x)$ (d) $b\left(\dfrac{x}{3}\right)$ (e) $a(x + 1)$ (f) $b(x + h)$

   (g) $b(x - h)$ (h) $a(b(x))$ (i) $b(a(x))$

4. Find the inverse of each of the following functions:

   (a) $f(x) = \pi - x$ (b) $h(t) = \dfrac{t}{3} + 2$ (c) $r(n) = \dfrac{1}{n}$ (d) $r(n) = \dfrac{1}{n - 1}$

   (e) $r(n) = \dfrac{2}{n - 1}$ (f) $r(n) = \dfrac{a}{n - b}$ where a and b are constants

5. Given $A(n) = n^2 + n - 6$ find expressions for
   (a) $A(n + 1)$ (b) $A(n - 1)$
   (c) $2A(n + 1) - A(n) + A(n - 1)$

6. Find $h^{-1}(x)$ when $h(x)$ is given by

   (a) $\dfrac{x + 1}{3}$ (b) $\dfrac{3}{x + 1}$ (c) $\dfrac{x + 1}{x}$ (d) $\dfrac{x}{x + 1}$

7. Given $v(t) = 4t - 2$ find
   (a) $v^{-1}(t)$ (b) $v(v(t))$

8. Given $h(x) = 9x - 6$ and $g(x) = \dfrac{1}{3x}$ find

    (a) $h(g(x))$ (b) $g(h(x))$

9. Given $f(x) = (x + 1)^2$, $g(x) = 4x$ and $h(x) = x - 1$ find

    (a) $f(g(x))$ (b) $g(f(x))$ (c) $f(h(x))$ (d) $h(f(x))$ (e) $g(h(x))$
    (f) $h(g(x))$ (g) $f(g(h(x)))$ (h) $g(h(f(x)))$

10. Given $x(t) = t^3$, $y(t) = \dfrac{1}{t+1}$ and $z(t) = 3t - 1$ find

    (a) $y(x(t))$ (b) $y(z(t))$ (c) $x(y(z(t)))$ (d) $z(y(x(t)))$

11. Write each of the following functions using mathematical notation:

    (a) The input is multiplied by 7.
    (b) Five times the square of the input is subtracted from twice the cube of the input.
    (c) The output is 6.
    (d) The input is added to the reciprocal of the input.
    (e) The input is multiplied by 11 and then 6 is subtracted from this. Finally, 9 is divided by
        this result.

12. Find the inverse of

    $$f(x) = \frac{x+1}{x-1}$$

The straight line

Objectives : This chapter:

- describes some special properties of straight line graphs
- explains the equation $y = mx + c$
- explains the terms 'vertical intercept' and 'gradient'
- shows how the equation of a line can be calculated
- explains what is meant by a tangent to a curve
- explains what is meant by the gradient of a curve
- explains how the gradient of a curve can be estimated by drawing a tangent

18.1 Straight line graphs

In the previous chapter we explained how to draw graphs of functions. Several of the resulting graphs were straight lines. In this chapter we focus specifically on the straight line and some of its properties.

Any equation of the form $y = mx + c$, where m and c are constants, will have a straight line graph. For example,

$$y = 3x + 7 \qquad y = -2x + \frac{1}{2} \qquad y = 3x - 1.5$$

will all result in straight line graphs. It is important to note that the variable x only occurs to the power 1. The values of m and c may be zero, so that $y = -3x$ is a straight line for which the value of c is zero, and $y = 17$ is a straight line for which the value of m is zero.

Key point

Any straight line has an equation of the form $y = mx + c$ where m and c are constants.

18.1   Which of the following equations have straight line graphs? For those that do, identify the values of m and c.

(a) $y = 7x + 5$ (b) $y = \dfrac{13x - 5}{2}$ (c) $y = 3x^2 + x$ (d) $y = -19$

Solution   (a) $y = 7x + 5$ is an equation of the form $y = mx + c$ where $m = 7$ and $c = 5$. This equation has a straight line graph.

(b) The equation

$$y = \frac{13x - 5}{2}$$

can be written as $y = \frac{13}{2}x - \frac{5}{2}$, which is in the form $y = mx + c$ with $m = \frac{13}{2}$ and $c = -\frac{5}{2}$. This has a straight line graph.

(c) $y = 3x^2 + x$ contains the term x^2. Such a term is not allowed in the equation of a straight line. The graph will not be a straight line.

(d) $y = -19$ is in the form of the equation of a straight line for which $m = 0$ and $c = -19$.

18.2   Plot each of the following graphs: $y = 2x + 3$, $y = 2x + 1$ and $y = 2x - 2$. Comment upon the resulting lines.

Solution   The three graphs are shown in Figure 18.1. Note that all three graphs have the same steepness or **slope**. However, each one cuts the vertical

Figure 18.1
Graphs of $y = 2x + 3$,
$y = 2x + 1$ and
$y = 2x - 2$

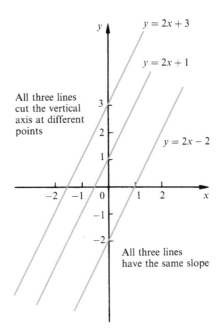

axis at a different point. This point can be obtained directly from the equation $y = 2x + c$ by looking at the value of c. For example, $y = 2x + 1$ intersects the vertical axis at $y = 1$. The graph of $y = 2x + 3$ cuts the vertical axis at $y = 3$, and the graph of $y = 2x - 2$ cuts this axis at $y = -2$.

The point where a graph cuts the vertical axis is called the **vertical intercept**. The vertical intercept can be obtained from $y = mx + c$ by looking at the value of c.

Key point

In the equation $y = mx + c$ the value of c gives the y coordinate of the point where the line cuts the vertical axis.

WORKED EXAMPLE

18.3   On the same graph plot the following: $y = x + 2$, $y = 2x + 2$, $y = 3x + 2$. Comment upon the graphs.

Solution   The three straight lines are shown in Figure 18.2. Note that the steepness of the line is determined by the coefficient of x, with $y = 3x + 2$ being steeper than $y = 2x + 2$, and this in turn being steeper than $y = x + 2$.

Figure 18.2
Graphs of $y = x + 2$,
$y = 2x + 2$, and
$y = 3x + 2$

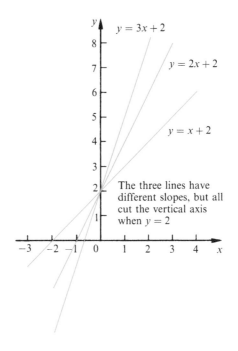

The three lines have different slopes, but all cut the vertical axis when $y = 2$

The value of m in the equation $y = mx + c$ determines the steepness of the straight line. The larger the value of m, the steeper is the line. The value m is known as the slope or **gradient** of the straight line.

Key point   In the equation $y = mx + c$ the value m is known as the gradient and is a measure of the steepness of the line.

If m is positive, the line will rise as we move from left to right. If m is negative, the line will fall. If $m = 0$ the line will be horizontal. We say it has zero gradient. These points are summarised in Figure 18.3.

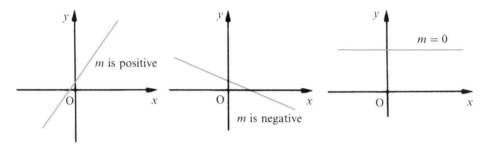

Figure 18.3
Straight line graphs with positive, negative and zero gradients

Self-assessment questions 18.1

1. Give the standard form of the equation of a straight line.

2. Explain the meaning of m and c in the equation $y = mx + c$.

Exercise 18.1

1. Identify, without plotting, which of the following functions will give straight line graphs:
   (a) $y = 3x + 9$ (b) $y = -9x + 2$ (c) $y = -6x$ (d) $y = x^2 + 3x$
   (e) $y = 17$ (f) $y = x^{-1} + 7$

2. Identify the gradient and vertical intercept of each of the following lines:
   (a) $y = 9x - 11$ (b) $y = 8x + 1.4$ (c) $y = \frac{1}{2}x - 11$ (d) $y = 17 - 2x$
   (e) $y = \dfrac{2x + 1}{3}$ (f) $y = \dfrac{4 - 2x}{5}$ (g) $y = 3(x - 1)$ (h) $y = 4$

3. Identify (i) the gradient and (ii) the vertical intercept of the following lines:
   (a) $y + x = 6$ (b) $y - 2x + 1 = 0$ (c) $2y - 4x + 3 = 0$ (d) $3x - 4y + 12 = 0$
   (e) $3x + \dfrac{y}{2} - 9 = 0$

18.2 Finding the equation of a straight line from its graph

If we are given the graph of a straight line it is often necessary to find its equation, $y = mx + c$. This amounts to finding the values of m and c. Finding the vertical intercept is straightforward because we can look directly for the point where the line cuts the y axis. The y coordinate of this point gives the value of c. The gradient m can be determined from knowledge of any two points on the line using the formula

Key point

$$\text{gradient} = \frac{\text{difference between the } y \text{ coordinates}}{\text{difference between the } x \text{ coordinates}}$$

WORKED EXAMPLES

18.4   A straight line graph is shown in Figure 18.4. Determine its equation.

Figure 18.4
Graph for Worked Example 18.4

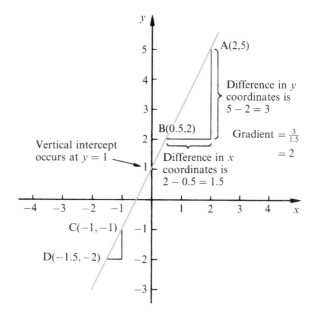

Solution   We require the equation of the line in the form $y = mx + c$. From the graph it is easy to see that the vertical intercept occurs at $y = 1$. Therefore the value of c is 1. To find the gradient m we choose any two points on the line. We have chosen the point A with coordinates (2, 5) and the point B with coordinates (0.5, 2). The difference between their y coordinates is then

$5 - 2 = 3$. The difference between their x coordinates is $2 - 0.5 = 1.5$. Then

$$\text{gradient} = \frac{\text{difference between their } y \text{ coordinates}}{\text{difference between their } x \text{ coordinates}}$$

$$= \frac{3}{1.5} = 2$$

The gradient m is equal to 2. Note that as we move from left to right the line is rising and so the value of m is positive. The equation of the line is then $y = 2x + 1$. There is nothing special about the points A and B. Any two points are sufficient to find m. For example, using the points C with coordinates $(-1, -1)$ and D with coordinates $(-1.5, -2)$ we would find

$$\text{gradient} = \frac{\text{difference between their } y \text{ coordinates}}{\text{difference between their } x \text{ coordinates}}$$

$$= \frac{-1 - (-2)}{-1 - (-1.5)}$$

$$= \frac{1}{0.5} = 2$$

as before.

18.5   A straight line graph is shown in Figure 18.5. Find its equation.

Figure 18.5
Graph for Worked
Example 18.5

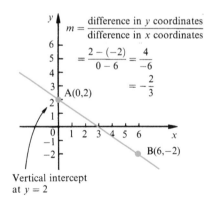

Vertical intercept
at $y = 2$

Solution   We need to find the equation in the form $y = mx + c$. From the graph we see immediately that the value of c is 2. To find the gradient we have selected any two points, A(0, 2) and B(6, −2). The difference between their y coordinates is $2 - (-2) = 4$. The difference between their x coordinates is $0 - 6 = -6$. Then

$$\text{gradient} = \frac{\text{difference between their } y \text{ coordinates}}{\text{difference between their } x \text{ coordinates}}$$

$$= \frac{4}{-6}$$

$$= -\frac{2}{3}$$

The equation of the line is therefore $y = -\frac{2}{3}x + 2$. Note in particular that, because the line is sloping downwards as we move from left to right, the gradient is negative. Note also that the coordinates of A and B both satisfy the equation of the line. That is, for A(0, 2),

$$2 = -\frac{2}{3}(0) + 2$$

and for B(6, −2),

$$-2 = -\frac{2}{3}(6) + 2$$

The coordinates of any other point on the line must also satisfy the equation.

The point noted at the end of Worked Example 18.5 is important:

Key point   If the point (a, b) lies on the line $y = mx + c$ then this equation is satisfied by letting $x = a$ and $y = b$.

WORKED EXAMPLE

18.6   Find the equation of the line shown in Figure 18.6.

Figure 18.6
Graph for Worked
Example 18.6

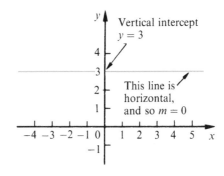

Solution   We are required to express the equation in the form $y = mx + c$. From the graph we notice that the line is horizontal. This means that its gradient is 0, that is $m = 0$. Furthermore the line cuts the vertical axis at $y = 3$ and so the equation of the line is $y = 0x + 3$ or simply $y = 3$.

It is not necessary to sketch a graph in order to find the equation. Consider the following worked examples, which illustrate an algebraic method.

WORKED EXAMPLES

18.7   A straight line passes through A(7, 1) and B(−3, 2). Find its equation.

Solution   The equation must be of the form $y = mx + c$. The gradient of the line can be found from

$$\text{gradient} = m = \frac{\text{difference between their } y \text{ coordinates}}{\text{difference between their } x \text{ coordinates}}$$

$$= \frac{1 - 2}{7 - (-3)}$$

$$= \frac{-1}{10}$$

$$= -0.1$$

Hence $y = -0.1x + c$. We can find c by noting that the line passes through (7, 1), that is the point where $x = 7$ and $y = 1$. Substituting these values into the equation $y = -0.1x + c$ gives

$$1 = -0.1(7) + c$$

so that $c = 1 + 0.7 = 1.7$. Therefore the equation of the line is $y = -0.1x + 1.7$.

18.8   Determine the equation of the line that passes through (4, −1) and has gradient −2.

Solution   Let the equation of the line be $y = mx + c$. We are told that the gradient of the line is −2, that is $m = -2$, and so we have

$$y = -2x + c$$

The point (4, −1) lies on this line: hence when $x = 4$, $y = -1$. These values are substituted into the equation of the line:

$$-1 = -2(4) + c$$

$$c = 7$$

The equation of the line is thus $y = -2x + 7$.

Self-assessment questions 18.2

1. State the formula for finding the gradient of a straight line when two points upon it are known. If the two points are (x_1, y_1) and (x_2, y_2) write down an expression for the gradient.

2. Explain how the value of c in the equation $y = mx + c$ can be found by inspecting the straight line graph.

Exercise 18.2

1. A straight line passes through the two points (1, 7) and (2, 9). Sketch a graph of the line and find its equation.

2. Find the equation of the line that passes through the two points (2, 2) and (3, 8).

3. Find the equation of the line that passes through (8, 2) and (−2, 2).

4. Find the equation of the straight line that has gradient 1 and passes through the origin.

5. Find the equation of the straight line that has gradient −1 and passes through the origin.

6. Find the equation of the straight line passing through (−1, 6) with gradient 2.

7. Which of the following points lie on the line $y = 4x - 3$?
   (a) (1, 2) (b) (2, 5) (c) (5, 17)
   (d) (−1, −7) (e) (0, 2)

8. Find the equation of the straight line passing through (−3, 7) with gradient −1.

9. Determine the equation of the line passing through (−1, −6) that is parallel to the line $y = 3x + 17$.

10. Find the equation of the line with vertical intercept −2 passing through (3, 10).

18.3 Gradients of tangents to curves

Figure 18.7 shows a graph of $y = x^2$. If you study the graph you will notice that as we move from left to right, at some points the y values are decreasing, whereas at others the y values are increasing. It is intuitively obvious that the slope of the curve changes from point to point. At some points, such as A, the curve appears quite steep and falling. At points such as B the curve appears quite steep and rising. Unlike a straight line, the slope of a curve is not fixed but changes as we move from one point to another. A useful way of measuring the slope at any point is to draw a **tangent** to the curve at that point. The tangent is a straight line that just touches the curve at the point of interest. In Figure 18.7 a tangent to the curve $y = x^2$ has been drawn at the point (2, 4). If we calculate the

Figure 18.7

A graph of $y = x^2$

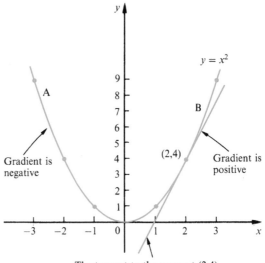

The tangent to the curve at (2,4)

gradient of this tangent, this gives the gradient of the curve at the point (2, 4).

Key point

The gradient of a curve at any point is equal to the gradient of the tangent at that point.

WORKED EXAMPLE

18.9

(a) Plot a graph of $y = x^2 - x$ for values of x between -2 and 4.

(b) Draw in tangents at the points A($-1, 2$) and B($3, 6$).

(c) By calculating the gradients of these tangents find the gradient of the curve at A and at B.

Solution

(a) A table of values and the graph are shown in Figure 18.8.

(b) We now draw tangents at A and B. At present, the best we can do is estimate these by eye.

(c) We now calculate the gradient of the tangent at A. We select any two points on the tangent and calculate the difference between their y coordinates and the difference between their x coordinates. We have chosen the points $(-3, 8)$ and $(-2, 5)$. Referring to Figure 18.8 we see that

$$\text{gradient of tangent at A} = \frac{8 - 5}{-3 - (-2)} = \frac{3}{-1}$$

$$= -3$$

Figure 18.8
A graph of $y = x^2 - x$

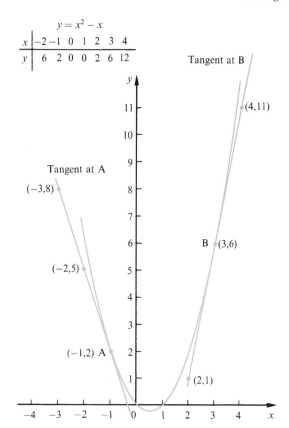

$$y = x^2 - x$$

x	-2	-1	0	1	2	3	4
y	6	2	0	0	2	6	12

Tangent at B

Tangent at A

Clearly, the accuracy of our answer depends to a great extent upon how well we can draw and measure the gradient of the tangent.

WORKED EXAMPLE

18.10   (a) Sketch a graph of the curve $y = x^3$ for $-2 \leqslant x \leqslant 2$.

(b) Draw the tangent to the graph at the point where $x = 1$.

(c) Estimate the gradient of this tangent and find its equation.

Solution   (a) A graph is shown in Figure 18.9.

Figure 18.9
Graph of $y = x^3$

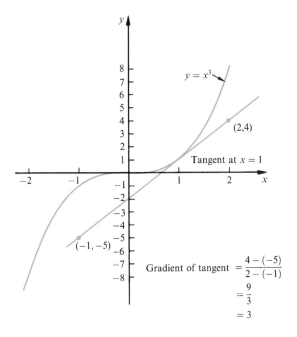

(b) The tangent has been drawn at $x = 1$.

(c) Let us write the equation of the tangent as $y = mx + c$. Two points on the tangent have been selected in order to estimate the gradient. These are $(2, 4)$ and $(-1, -5)$. From these we find

$$\text{gradient of tangent is approximately } \frac{4 - (-5)}{2 - (-1)} = \frac{9}{3} = 3$$

Therefore $m = 3$. The value of c is found by noting that the vertical intercept of the tangent is -2. The equation of the tangent is then $y = 3x - 2$.

Of course, this method will usually result in an approximation based upon how well we have drawn the graph and its tangent. A much more precise method for calculating gradients of curves is given in Chapter 33.

Self-assessment questions 18.3

1. Explain what is meant by the 'tangent' to a curve at a point.

2. Explain how a tangent is used to determine the gradient of a curve.

Exercise 18.3

1. Draw the graph of $y = 2x^2 - 1$ for values of x between -3 and 3. By drawing a tangent, estimate the gradient of the curve at A(2, 7) and B(-1, 1).

2. Draw the graph of $y = -2x^2 + 2$ for values of x between -3 and 3. Draw the tangent at the point where $x = 1$ and calculate its equation.

Test and assignment exercises 18

1. Which of the following will have straight line graphs?

   (a) $y = 2x - 11$ (b) $y = 5x + 10$ (c) $y = x^2 - 1$ (d) $y = -3 + 3x$ (e) $y = \dfrac{2x + 3}{2}$

   For each straight line, identify the gradient and vertical intercept.

2. Find the equation of the straight line that passes through the points (1, 11) and (2, 18). Show that the line also passes through $(-1, -3)$.

3. Find the equation of the line that has gradient -2 and passes through the point (1, 1).

4. Find the equation of the line that passes through $(-1, 5)$ and (1, 5). Does the line also pass through (2, 6)?

5. Draw a graph of $y = -x^2 + 3x$ for values of x between -3 and 3. By drawing in tangents estimate the gradient of the curve at the points $(-2, -10)$ and (1, 2).

6. Find the equations of the lines passing through the origin with gradients (a) -2, (b) -4, (c) 4.

7. Find the equation of the line passing through (4, 10) and parallel to $y = 6x - 3$.

8. Find the equation of the line with vertical intercept 3 and passing through $(-1, 9)$.

9. Find where the line joining $(-2, 4)$ and (3, 10) cuts (a) the x axis, (b) the y axis.

10. A line cuts the x axis at $x = -2$ and the y axis at $y = 3$. Determine the equation of the line.

11. Determine where the line $y = 4x - 1$ cuts
    (a) the y axis   (b) the x axis   (c) the line $y = 2$

Tables and charts

Objectives : This chapter:

- explains the distinction between discrete and continuous data
- shows how raw data can be organised using a tally chart
- explains what is meant by a frequency distribution and a relative frequency distribution
- shows how data can be represented in the form of bar charts, pie charts, pictograms and histograms

28.1 Introduction to data

In the modern world, information from a wide range of sources is gathered, presented and interpreted. Most newspapers, television news programmes and documentaries contain vast numbers of facts and figures concerning almost every aspect of life, including environmental issues, the lengths of hospital waiting lists, crime statistics and economic performance indicators. Information such as this, which is gathered by carrying out surveys and doing research, is known as **data**.

Sometimes data must take on a value from a specific set of numbers, and no other values are possible. For example, the number of children in a family must be 0, 1, 2, 3, 4 and so on, and no intermediate values are allowed. It is impossible to have 3.32 children, say. Usually one allowable value differs from the next by a fixed amount. Such data is said to be **discrete**. Other examples of discrete data include:

- the number of car thefts in a city in one week – this must be 0, 1, 2, 3 and so on. You cannot have three-and-a-half thefts.
- shoe sizes – these can be ..., $3\frac{1}{2}$, 4, $4\frac{1}{2}$, 5, $5\frac{1}{2}$, 6, $6\frac{1}{2}$, 7 and so on. You cannot have a shoe size of 9.82.

Sometimes data can take on *any* value within a specified range. Such data is called **continuous**. The volume of liquid in a 1 litre jug can take any value from 0 to 1 litre. The lifespan of an electric light bulb could be any non-negative value.

Frequently data is presented in the form of tables and charts, the intention being to make the information readily understandable. When data is first collected, and before it is processed in any way, it is known as **raw data**. For example, in a test the mathematics marks out of 10 of a group of 30 students are

7	5	5	8	9	10	9	10	7	8	6	3	5	9	6
10	8	8	7	8	6	7	8	8	10	9	4	5	9	8

This is raw data. To try to make sense of this data it is helpful to find out how many students scored each particular mark. This can be done by means of a **tally chart**. To produce this we write down in a column all the possible marks, in order. We then go through the raw data and indicate the occurrence of each mark with a vertical line or tally like /. Every time a fifth tally is recorded this is shown by striking through the previous four, as in ⫻⫻. This makes counting up the tallies particularly easy. The tallies for all the marks are shown in Table 28.1. The number of occurrences of each mark is called its **frequency**, and the frequencies can be found from the number of tallies. We see that the tally chart is a useful way of organising the raw data into a form that will enable us to answer questions and obtain useful information about it.

Table 28.1
Tally chart for
mathematics marks

Mark	Tally	Frequency
0		0
1		0
2		0
3	/	1
4	/	1
5	////	4
6	///	3
7	////	4
8	⫻⫻ ///	8
9	⫻⫻	5
10	////	4
Total		30

Nowadays much of the tedium of producing tally charts for very large amounts of data can be avoided using computer programs available specifically for this purpose.

Self-assessment questions 28.1

1. Explain the distinction between discrete data and continuous data. Give a new example of each.

2. Explain the purpose of a tally chart.

Exercise 28.1

1. State whether each of the following is an example of discrete data or continuous data:
   (a) the number of matches found in a matchbox
   (b) the percentage of sulphur dioxide found in an air sample taken above a city
   (c) the number of peas in a packet of frozen peas
   (d) the radius of a ball bearing
   (e) the weight of a baby
   (f) the number of students in a particular type of accommodation
   (g) the weight of a soil sample
   (h) the temperature of a patient in hospital
   (i) the number of telephone calls received by an answering machine during one day

2. Twenty-five people were asked to state their year of birth. The information given was

   1975 1975 1974 1974 1975 1976 1976 1974 1972 1973 1973 1970 1975
   1975 1973 1970 1975 1974 1975 1974 1970 1973 1974 1974 1975

   Produce a tally chart to organise this data and state the frequency of occurrence of each year of birth.

28.2 Frequency tables and distributions

Data is often presented in a **table**. For example, in a recent survey, 1000 students were asked to state the type of accommodation in which they lived during term time. The data gathered is given in Table 28.2. As we saw from the work in the previous section, the number of occurrences of each entry in the table is known as its **frequency**. So, for example, the frequency of students in private rented accommodation is 250. The table summarises the various frequencies and is known as a **frequency distribution**.

A **relative frequency distribution** is found by expressing each frequency as a proportion of the total frequency.

Table 28.2
Frequency distribution

Type of accommodation	Number of students
Hall of residence	675
Parental home	50
Private rented	250
Other	25
Total	1000

Key point   The relative frequency is found by dividing a frequency by the total frequency.

In this example, because the total frequency is 1000, the relative frequency is easy to calculate. The number of students living at their parental home is 50 out of a total of 1000. Therefore the relative frequency of this group of students is $\frac{50}{1000}$ or 0.050. Table 28.3 shows the relative frequency distribution of student accommodation. Note that the relative frequencies always sum to 1.

Table 28.3
Relative frequency
distribution

Type of accommodation	Number of students	Relative frequency
Hall of residence	675	0.675
Parental home	50	0.050
Private rented	250	0.250
Other	25	0.025
Total	1000	1.000

It is sometimes helpful to express the frequencies as percentages. This is done by multiplying each relative frequency by 100, which gives the results shown in Table 28.4. We see from this that 5% of students questioned live at their parental home.

Table 28.4
Frequencies expressed as
percentages

Type of accommodation	Number of students	Relative frequency × 100
Hall of residence	675	67.5%
Parental home	50	5.0%
Private rented	250	25.0%
Other	25	2.5%
Total	1000	100%

| Key point | A frequency can be expressed as a percentage by multiplying its relative frequency by 100. |

WORKED EXAMPLE

28.1   In 1988 there were 4320 areas throughout the world that were designated as national parks. Table 28.5 is a frequency distribution showing how these parks are distributed in different parts of the world.

(a)   Express this data as a relative frequency distribution and also in terms of percentages.

(b)   What percentage of the world's national parks are in Africa?

Table 28.5
The number of national parks throughout the world

Region	Number of national parks
Africa	486
N. America	587
S. America	315
Former Soviet Union	168
Asia	960
Europe	1032
Oceania	767
Antarctica	5
Total	4320

Solution

Table 28.6
The number of national parks throughout the world

Region	Number	Relative frequency	Rel. freq. $\times$ 100
Africa	486	0.1125	11.25%
N. America	587	0.1359	13.59%
S. America	315	0.0729	7.29%
Former Soviet Union	168	0.0389	3.89%
Asia	960	0.2222	22.22%
Europe	1032	0.2389	23.89%
Oceania	767	0.1775	17.75%
Antarctica	5	0.0012	0.12%
Total	4320	1.000	100%

(a) The relative frequencies are found by expressing each frequency as a proportion of the total. For example, Europe has 1032 national parks out of a total of 4320, and so its relative frequency is $\frac{1032}{4320} = 0.2389$. Figures for the other regions have been calculated and are shown in Table 28.6. To express a relative frequency as a percentage it is multiplied by 100. Thus we find that Europe has 23.89% of the world's national parks. The percentages for the other regions are also shown in Table 28.6.

(b) We note from Table 28.6 that 11.25% of the world's national parks are in Africa.

When dealing with large amounts of data it is usual to group the data into classes. For example, in an environmental experiment the weights in grams of 30 soil samples were measured using a balance. We could list all 30 weights here but such a long list of data is cumbersome. Instead, we have already grouped the data into several weight ranges or **classes**. Table 28.7 shows the number of samples in each class. Such a table is called a **grouped frequency distribution**.

Table 28.7
Grouped frequency distribution

Weight range (grams)	Number of samples in that range
100–109	5
110–119	8
120–129	11
130–139	5
140–149	1
Total	30

A disadvantage of grouping the data in this way is that information about individual weights is lost. However, this disadvantage is usually outweighed by having a more compact set of data that is easier to work with. There are five samples that lie in the first class, eight samples in the second and so on. For the first class, the numbers 100 and 109 are called **class limits**, the smaller number being the **lower class limit** and the larger being the **upper class limit**. Theoretically, the class 100–109 includes all weights from 99.5 g up to but not including 109.5 g. These numbers are called the **class boundaries**. In practice the class boundaries are found by adding the upper class limit of one class to the lower limit of the next class and dividing by 2. The **class width** is the difference between the larger class boundary and the smaller. The class 100–109 has width $109.5 - 99.5 = 10$. We do not know the actual values of the weights in each class. Should we require an estimate, the best we can do is use the value in the middle of the class, known as the class **midpoint**. The midpoint of the first class is 104.5, the midpoint of the second class is 114.5 and so on. The midpoint can be found by adding half the class width to the lower class boundary.

WORKED EXAMPLE

28.2 The systolic blood pressure in millimetres of mercury of 20 workers was recorded to the nearest millimetre. The data collected was as follows:

121   123   124   129   130   119   129   124   119   121   122   124
124   128   129   136   120   119   121   136

(a) Group this data into classes 115–119, 120–124, and so on.
(b) State the class limits of the first three classes.
(c) State the class boundaries of the first three classes.
(d) What is the class width of the third class?
(e) What is the midpoint of the third class?

Solution (a) To group the data a tally chart is used as shown in Table 28.8.

Table 28.8
Tally chart for blood pressures

Pressure (mm mercury)	Tally	Frequency
115–119	///	3
120–124	ЖЖ ЖЖ	10
125–129	////	4
130–134	/	1
135–139	//	2
Total		20

(b) The class limits of the first class are 115 and 119; those of the second class are 120 and 124; those of the third are 125 and 129.

(c) Theoretically, the class 115–119 will contain all blood pressures between 114.5 and 119.5 and so the class boundaries of the first class are 114.5 and 119.5. The class boundaries of the second class are 119.5 and 124.5, and those of the third class are 124.5 and 129.5.

(d) The upper class boundary of the third class is 129.5. The lower class boundary is 124.5. The difference between these values gives the class width, that is 129.5 – 124.5 = 5.

(e) The midpoint of the third class is found by adding half the class width to the lower class boundary, that is 2.5 + 124.5 = 127.

Self-assessment questions 28.2

1. Why is it often useful to present data in the form of a *grouped* frequency distribution?

2. Explain the distinction between class boundaries and class limits.

3. How is the class width calculated?

4. How is the class midpoint calculated?

Exercise 28.2

1. The age of each patient over the age of 14 visiting a doctor's practice in one day was recorded as follows:

   18 18 76 15 72 45 48 62 21
   27 45 43 28 19 17 37 35 34
   23 25 46 56 32 18 23 34 32
   56 29 43

   (a) Use a tally chart to produce a grouped frequency distribution with age groupings 15–19, 20–24, 25–29, and so on.
   (b) What is the relative frequency of patients in the age group 70–74?
   (c) What is the relative frequency of patients aged 70 and over?
   (d) Express the number of patients in the age group 25–29 as a percentage.

2. Consider the following table, which shows the lifetimes, to the nearest hour, of 100 energy saving light bulbs.

   (a) If a light bulb has a life of 5499.4 hours into which class will it be put?
   (b) If a light bulb has a life of 5499.8 hours into which class will it be put?
   (c) State the class boundaries of each class.

   (d) Find the class width.
   (e) State the class midpoint of each class.

Lifetime (hours)	Frequency
5000–5499	6
5500–5999	32
6000–6499	58
6500–6999	4
Total	100

3. The percentages of 60 students in an Information Technology test are given as follows:

   45 92 81 76 51 46 82 65 61
   19 62 58 72 65 66 97 61 57
   63 93 61 46 47 61 56 45 39
   47 55 58 81 71 52 38 53 59
   82 92 87 86 51 29 19 79 55
   18 53 29 87 87 77 85 67 89
   17 29 86 57 59 57

   Form a frequency distribution by drawing up a tally chart using class intervals 0–9, 10–19 and so on.

4. The data in the table opposite gives the radius of 20 ball bearings. State the class boundaries of the second class and find the class width.

Radius (mm)	Frequency
20.56–20.58	3
20.59–20.61	6
20.62–20.64	8
20.65–20.67	3

28.3 Bar charts, pie charts, pictograms and histograms

In a **bar chart** information is represented by rectangles or bars. The bars may be drawn horizontally or vertically. The length of each bar corresponds to a frequency.

The data given earlier in Table 28.2 concerning student accommodation is presented in the form of a horizontal bar chart in Figure 28.1. Note that the scale on the horizontal axis must be uniform, that is it must be evenly spaced, and that the type of accommodation is clearly identified on each bar. The bar chart must be given a title to explain the information that is being presented.

Figure 28.1
Horizontal bar chart showing student accommodation

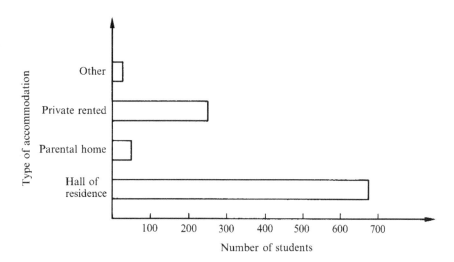

WORKED EXAMPLE

28.3   A reproduction antique furniture manufacturer has been producing pine wardrobes for the past six years. The number of wardrobes sold each year is given in Table 28.9. Produce a vertical bar chart to illustrate this information.

Table 28.9
Wardrobes sold

Year	Number sold
2003	15
2004	16
2005	20
2006	20
2007	24
2008	30

Solution   The information is presented in the form of a vertical bar chart in Figure 28.2.

Figure 28.2
Vertical bar chart showing the number of wardrobes sold each year

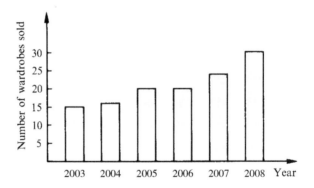

In a **pie chart**, a circular 'pie' is divided into a number of portions, with each portion, or **sector**, of the pie representing a different category. The whole pie represents all categories together. The size of a particular portion must represent the number in its category, and this is done by dividing the circle proportionately. Usually a protractor will be required.

WORKED EXAMPLE

28.4   A sample of 360 people were asked to state their favourite flavour of potato crisp: 75 preferred 'plain' crisps, 120 preferred 'cheese and onion',

90 preferred 'salt and vinegar', and the remaining 75 preferred 'beef'. Draw a pie chart to present this data.

Solution   All categories together, that is all 360 people asked, make up the whole pie. Because there are 360° in a circle this makes the pie chart particularly easy to draw. A sector of angle 75° will represent 'plain crisps', a sector of 120° will represent 'cheese and onion' and so on. The pie chart is shown in Figure 28.3.

Figure 28.3
Pie chart showing preferred flavour of crisps of 360 people

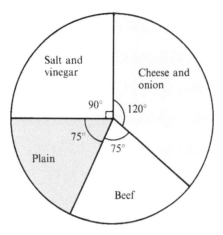

The pie chart in the previous worked example was simple to draw because the total number of all categories was 360, the same as the number of degrees in a circle. Let us now see how to deal with a situation where this is not the case. First each relative frequency is found and then this is multiplied by 360. The result is the angle, in degrees, of the corresponding sector.

Key point   The angle, in degrees, of each sector in a pie chart is found by multiplying the corresponding relative frequency by 360. This gives the angle of each sector.

WORKED EXAMPLE

28.5   Five hundred students were asked to state how they usually travelled to and from their place of study. The results are given in Table 28.10. Present this information in a pie chart.

Solution   To find the angle of each sector of the pie chart we first find the corresponding relative frequencies. Recall that this is done by dividing each frequency by the total, 500. Then each relative frequency is multiplied by 360. The results are shown in Table 28.11. The table gives the required

Table 28.10
Means of travel

Means of travel	Frequency f
Bus	50
Walk	180
Cycle	200
Car	40
Other	30
Total	500

Table 28.11
Means of travel

Means of travel	Frequency f	Rel. freq. $f/500$	Rel. freq. $\times 360$
Bus	50	$\frac{50}{500}$	$\frac{50}{500} \times 360 = 36.0°$
Walk	180	$\frac{180}{500}$	$\frac{180}{500} \times 360 = 129.6°$
Cycle	200	$\frac{200}{500}$	$\frac{200}{500} \times 360 = 144.0°$
Car	40	$\frac{40}{500}$	$\frac{40}{500} \times 360 = 28.8°$
Other	30	$\frac{30}{500}$	$\frac{30}{500} \times 360 = 21.6°$
Total	500		360°

Figure 28.4
Pie chart showing how
students travel to work

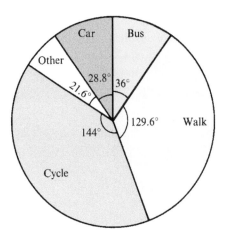

angles. Using a protractor the pie chart can then be drawn. This is shown
in Figure 28.4.

A **pictogram** uses a picture to represent data in an eye-catching way.
There are many ways to produce pictograms but generally the number of
objects drawn represents the number of items in a particular category. This

is a common form of representation popular on television when the viewer sees the information for only a few seconds.

WORKED EXAMPLE

28.6   The number of hours of sunshine in the month of August 1975 in four popular holiday resorts is given in Table 28.12. Show this information using a pictogram. Use one 'sun' to represent 100 hours of sunshine.

Table 28.12
Hours of sunshine in August 1975 in four resorts

Resort	Number of hours
Torbay	300
Scarborough	275
Blackpool	350
Brighton	325

Solution   The pictogram is shown in Figure 28.5.

Figure 28.5
Pictogram showing hours of sunshine in August 1975

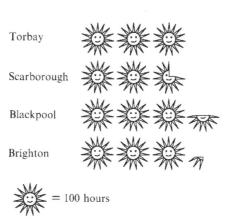

A **histogram** is often used to illustrate data that is continuous or has been grouped. It is similar to a vertical bar chart in that it is drawn by constructing vertical rectangles. However, in a histogram it is the *area* of each rectangle, and not its length, that is proportional to the frequency of each class. When all class widths are the same this point is not important and you can assume that the length of a rectangle represents the frequency. Class boundaries and not class limits must be used on the horizontal axis to distinguish one class from the next. Consider the following example.

WORKED EXAMPLE

28.7   The heights, to the nearest centimetre, of 100 students are given in Table 28.13.

Table 28.13
Height of 100 students

Height (cm)	Frequency
164–165	4
166–167	8
168–169	10
170–171	27
172–173	30
174–175	10
176–177	6
178–179	5
Total	100

(a) State the class limits of the second class.

(b) Identify the class boundaries of the first class and the last class.

(c) In which class would a student whose actual height is 167.4 cm be placed?

(d) In which class would a student whose actual height is 167.5 cm be placed?

(e) Draw a histogram to depict this data.

Solution   (a) The lower class limit of the second class is 166 cm. The upper class limit is 167 cm.

(b) The class boundaries of the first class are 163.5 cm and 165.5 cm. The class boundaries of the last class are 177.5 cm and 179.5 cm.

(c) A student with height 167.4 cm will have his height recorded to the nearest centimetre as 167. He will be placed in the class 166–167.

(d) A student with height 167.5 cm will have her height recorded to the nearest centimetre as 168. She will be placed in the class 168–169.

(e) The histogram is shown in Figure 28.6. Note that the class boundaries are used on the horizontal axis to distinguish one class from the next. The area of each rectangle is proportional to the frequency of each class.

Figure 28.6
Histogram showing the
distribution of heights of
100 students

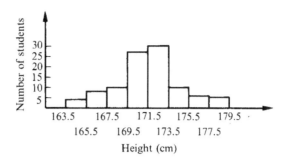

Self-assessment questions 28.3

1. There is an important distinction between a histogram and a vertical bar chart. Can you explain this?

2. Give one advantage and one disadvantage of using a pictogram to represent data.

3. On a histogram the class boundaries are used on the horizontal axis to distinguish one class from the next. Why do you think class boundaries as opposed to class limits are used?

Exercise 28.3

MyMathLab

1. A local council wants to produce a leaflet explaining how the council tax is spent. For every one pound spent, 40p went to Education, 15p went to the Police, 15p went to Cleansing and Refuse, 20p went to Highways and the remaining 10p went to a variety of other services. Show this information (a) using a pie chart, and (b) using a pictogram.

2. The composition of the atmosphere of the Earth is 78% nitrogen, 21% oxygen and 1% other gases. Draw a pie chart to show this information.

3. An insurance company keeps records on the distribution of the amount of small claims for theft it receives. Amounts are given to the nearest pound. This information is given in the following table.

Amount (£)	Frequency
0–99	5
100–199	8
200–299	16
300–399	24
400–499	26

(a) State the class boundaries.
(b) In which class would a claim for £199.75 be placed?
(c) Draw a histogram to show this information.

1. State whether the following are examples of discrete or continuous data:

    (a) the temperature of a furnace
    (b) the number of goals scored in a football match
    (c) the amount of money in a worker's wage packet at the end of the week

2. A group of students were interviewed to obtain information on their termly expenditure. On average, for every pound spent, 60p was spent on accommodation, fuel etc., 25p was spent on food, 10p was spent on entertainment and the remainder on a variety of other items. Draw a pie chart to show this expenditure.

3. Forty lecturers were asked to state which newspaper they bought most regularly. The results were: *Guardian*, 15; *Independent*, 8; *The Times*, 2; *Daily Express*, 7; *Daily Mail*, 2; None, 6. Produce a pie chart to show this data.

4. The percentage of total body weight formed by various parts of the body of a newborn baby is as follows: muscles, 26%; skeleton, 17%; skin, 20%; heart, lungs etc., 11%; remainder, 26%. Depict this information (a) on a pie chart, (b) using a bar chart.

5. The following marks were obtained by 27 students in a test. Draw up a frequency distribution by means of a tally chart.

    5 4 6 2 9 1 10 10 5 5 6 5 5 9 8 7 9 6 7 6 8 7 6 9 8 8 7

6. The number of cars sold by a major manufacturer of luxury cars in the last 10 years is given in the table below. Show this data on a horizontal bar chart.

Year	Number
1999	2000
2000	2320
2001	2380
2002	2600
2003	2650
2004	2750
2005	2750
2006	2800
2007	1500
2008	1425

7. The table below shows the frequency distribution of the lifetimes in hours of 100 light bulbs tested.

    (a) State the class limits of the first and second classes.

(b) State the class boundaries of all classes.
(c) Determine each class width and midpoint.
(d) Draw a histogram for this frequency distribution.

Lifetime (hours)	Frequency
600–699	13
700–799	25
800–899	32
900–999	10
1000–1099	15
1100–1199	5

8. In each year from 1988 to 1993 the numbers of visitors to a museum were respectively 12000, 13000, 14500, 18000, 18000 and 17500. Show this information in a pictogram.

Statistics

29.1 Introduction

In the previous chapter we outlined how data gathered from a range of sources can be represented. In order to get the most out of such data and be able to interpret it sensibly and reliably, techniques have been developed for its analysis. **Statistics** is the name given to this science. One important statistical quantity is an 'average', the purpose of which is to represent a whole set of data by a single number that in some way represents the set. This chapter explains three types of average and shows how to calculate them. Finally the 'variance' and 'standard deviation' are introduced. These are numbers that describe how widely the data is spread.

29.2 Averages: the mean, median and mode

When presented with a large amount of data it is often useful to ask 'is there a single number that typifies the data?' For example, following an examination taken by a large number of candidates, examiners may be dealing with hundreds of examination scripts. The marks on these will vary from those with very poor marks to those with very high or even top marks. In order to judge whether the group of students as a whole found the examination difficult, the examiner may be asked to provide a single value that gives a measure of how well the students have performed. Such a value is called an **average**. In statistics there are three important averages: the arithmetic mean, the median and the mode.

The arithmetic mean

The **arithmetic mean**, or simply the **mean**, of a set of values is found by adding up all the values and dividing the result by the total number of values in the set. It is given by the following formula:

Key point

$$\text{mean} = \frac{\text{sum of the values}}{\text{total number of values}}$$

WORKED EXAMPLES

29.1   Eight students sit a mathematics test and their marks out of 10 are 4, 6, 6, 7, 7, 7, 8 and 10. Find the mean mark.

Solution   The sum of the marks is $4 + 6 + 6 + 7 + 7 + 7 + 8 + 10 = 55$. The total number of values is 8. Therefore,

$$\text{mean} = \frac{\text{sum of the values}}{\text{total number of values}} = \frac{55}{8} = 6.875$$

The examiner can quote 6.875 out of 10 as the 'average mark' of the group of students.

29.2   In a hospital a patient's body temperature is recorded every hour for six hours. Find the mean temperature over the six-hour period if the six temperatures, in °C, were

36.5   36.8   36.9   36.9   36.9   37.0

Solution   To find the mean temperature the sum of all six values is found and the result is divided by 6. That is,

$$\text{mean} = \frac{36.5 + 36.8 + 36.9 + 36.9 + 36.9 + 37.0}{6}$$

$$= \frac{221.0}{6} = 36.83 \text{ °C}$$

In more advanced work we make use of a formula for the mean that requires knowledge of some special notation. Suppose we have n values and we call these x_1, x_2, x_3 and so on up to x_n. The mean of these values is given the symbol $\bar{x}$, pronounced 'x bar'. To calculate the mean we must add up these values and divide by n, that is

$$\text{mean} = \bar{x} = \frac{x_1 + x_2 + x_3 + \cdots + x_n}{n}$$

A notation is often used to shorten this formula. In mathematics, the Greek letter sigma, written $\sum$, stands for a sum. The sum $x_1 + x_2$ is written

$$\sum_{i=1}^{2} x_i$$

and the sum $x_1 + x_2 + x_3 + x_4$ is written

$$\sum_{i=1}^{4} x_i$$

Note that i runs through all integer values from 1 to n.

where the values above and below the sigma sign give the first and last values in the sum. Similarly $x_1 + x_2 + x_3 + \cdots + x_n$ is written $\sum_{i=1}^{n} x_i$. Using this notation, the formula for the mean can be written in the following way:

Key point

$$\text{mean} = \bar{x} = \frac{\sum_{i=1}^{n} x_i}{n}$$

There is a further treatment of sigma notation in Chapter 12, §12.5.

WORKED EXAMPLES

29.3   Express the following in sigma notation:

(a) $x_1 + x_2 + x_3 + \cdots + x_8 + x_9$ (b) $x_{10} + x_{11} + \cdots + x_{100}$

Solution   (a) $x_1 + x_2 + x_3 + \cdots + x_8 + x_9 = \sum_{i=1}^{9} x_i$

(b) $x_{10} + x_{11} + \cdots + x_{100} = \sum_{i=10}^{100} x_i$

29.4   Find the mean of the values $x_1 = 5$, $x_2 = 7$, $x_3 = 13$, $x_4 = 21$ and $x_5 = 29$.

Solution   The number of values equals 5, so we let $n = 5$. The sum of the values is

$$\sum_{i=1}^{5} x_i = x_1 + x_2 + x_3 + x_4 + x_5 = 5 + 7 + 13 + 21 + 29 = 75$$

The mean is

$$\text{mean} = \bar{x} = \frac{\sum_{i=1}^{5} x_i}{n} = \frac{75}{5} = 15$$

When the data is presented in the form of a frequency distribution the mean is found by first multiplying each data value by its frequency. The results are added. This is equivalent to adding up all the data values. The mean is found by dividing this sum by the sum of all the frequencies. Note that the sum of the frequencies is equal to the total number of values. Consider the following example.

WORKED EXAMPLE

29.5   Thirty-eight students sit a mathematics test and their marks out of 10 are shown in Table 29.1. Find the mean mark.

Solution   Each data value, in this case the mark, is multiplied by its frequency, and the results are added. This is equivalent to adding up all the 38 individual marks. This is shown in Table 29.2.

Table 29.1
Marks of 38 students in a test

Table 29.2
Marks of 38 students multiplied by frequency

Mark, m	Frequency, f	Mark, m	Frequency, f	$m \times f$
0	0	0	0	0
1	0	1	0	0
2	1	2	1	2
3	0	3	0	0
4	1	4	1	4
5	7	5	7	35
6	16	6	16	96
7	8	7	8	56
8	3	8	3	24
9	1	9	1	9
10	1	10	1	10
Total	38	Totals	38	236

Note that the sum of all the frequencies is equal to the number of students taking the test. The number 236 is equal to the sum of all the individual marks. The mean is found by dividing this sum by the sum of all the frequencies:

$$\text{mean} = \frac{236}{38} = 6.21$$

The mean mark is 6.21 out of 10.

Using the sigma notation the formula for the mean mark of a frequency distribution with N classes, where the frequency of value x_i is f_i, becomes

Key point

$$\text{mean} = \bar{x} = \frac{\sum_{i=1}^{N} f_i \times x_i}{\sum_{i=1}^{N} f_i}$$

Note that $\sum_{i=1}^{N} f_i = n$; that is, the sum of all the frequencies equals the total number of values.

When the data is in the form of a grouped distribution the class midpoint is used to calculate the mean. Consider the following example.

WORKED EXAMPLE

29.6   The heights, to the nearest centimetre, of 100 students are given in Table 29.3. Find the mean height.

Solution   Because the actual heights of students in each class are not known we use the midpoint of the class as an estimate. The midpoint of the class 164–165 is 164.5. Other midpoints and the calculation of the mean are shown in Table 29.4.

Then

$$\text{mean} = \bar{x} = \frac{\sum_{i=1}^{N} f_i \times x_i}{\sum_{i=1}^{N} f_i} = \frac{17150}{100} = 171.5$$

The mean height is 171.5 cm.

Table 29.3
Heights of 100 students

Height (cm)	Frequency
164–165	4
166–167	8
168–169	10
170–171	27
172–173	30
174–175	10
176–177	6
178–179	5
Total	100

Table 29.4
Heights of 100 students with midpoints multiplied by frequency

Height (cm)	Frequency f_i	Midpoint x_i	$f_i \times x_i$
164–165	4	164.5	658.0
166–167	8	166.5	1332.0
168–169	10	168.5	1685.0
170–171	27	170.5	4603.5
172–173	30	172.5	5175.0
174–175	10	174.5	1745.0
176–177	6	176.5	1059.0
178–179	5	178.5	892.5
Total	100		17150.0

The median

A second average that also typifies a set of data is the **median**.

The **median** of a set of numbers is found by listing the numbers in ascending order and then selecting the value that lies halfway along the list.

WORKED EXAMPLE

29.7   Find the median of the numbers

1   2   6   7   9   11   11   11   14

Solution   The set of numbers is already given in order. The number halfway along the list is 9, because there are four numbers before it and four numbers after it in the list. Hence the median is 9.

When there is an even number of values, the median is found by taking the mean of the two middle values.

WORKED EXAMPLE

29.8   Find the median of the following salaries: £24,000, £12,000, £16,000, £22,000, £10,000 and £25,000.

Solution   The numbers are first arranged in order as £10,000, £12,000, £16,000, £22,000, £24,000 and £25,000. Because there is an even number of values there are two middle figures: £16,000 and £22,000. The mean of these is

$$\frac{16,000 + 22,000}{2} = 19,000$$

The median salary is therefore £19,000.

The mode

A third average is the **mode**.

The **mode** of a set of values is that value that occurs most often.

WORKED EXAMPLE

29.9   Find the mode of the set of numbers

   1 1 4 4 5 6 8 8 8 9

Solution   The number that occurs most often is 8, which occurs three times. Therefore 8 is the mode. Usually a mode is quoted when we want to represent the most popular value in a set.

Sometimes a set of data may have more than one mode.

WORKED EXAMPLE

29.10   Find the mode of the set of numbers

   20   20   21   21   21   48   48   49   49   49

Solution   In this example there is no single value that occurs most frequently. The number 21 occurs three times, but so does the number 49. This set has two modes. The data is said to be **bimodal**.

Self-assessment questions 29.2

1. State the three different types of average commonly used in statistical calculations.

2. In an annual report, an employer of a small firm claims that the median salary for the workforce is £18,500. However, over discussions in the canteen it is apparent that no worker earns this amount. Explain how this might have arisen.

Exercise 29.2

1. Find the mean, median and mode of the following set of values: 2, 3, 5, 5, 5, 5, 8, 8, 9.

2. Find the mean of the set of numbers 1, 1, 1, 1, 1, 1, 256. Explain why the mean does not represent the data adequately. Which average might it have been more appropriate to use?

3. The marks of seven students in a test were 45%, 83%, 99%, 65%, 68%, 72% and 66%. Find the mean mark and the median mark.

4. Write out fully each of the following expressions:

   (a) $\sum_{i=1}^{4} x_i$ (b) $\sum_{i=1}^{7} x_i$

   (c) $\sum_{i=1}^{3} (x_i - 3)^2$ (d) $\sum_{i=1}^{4} (2 - x_i)^2$

5. Write the following concisely using sigma notation:
   (a) $x_3 + x_4 + x_5 + x_6$
   (b) $(x_1 - 1) + (x_2 - 1) + (x_3 - 1)$

6. Calculate the mean, median and mode of the following numbers: 1.00, 1.15, 1.25, 1.38, 1.39 and 1.40.

7. The prices of the eight executive homes advertised by a local estate agent are

£290,000 £375,000 £325,000 £299,950
£319,950 £327,500 £299,500 £329,500

Find the mean price of these houses.

8. The data in the table gives the radius of 20 ball bearings. Find the class midpoints and hence calculate the average radius.

Radius (mm)	Frequency
20.56–20.58	3
20.59–20.61	6
20.62–20.64	8
20.65–20.67	3

29.3 The variance and standard deviation

Suppose we consider the test marks of two groups of three students. Suppose that the marks out of 10 for the first group are

4   7   and   10

while those of the second group are

7   7   and   7

It is easy to calculate the mean mark of each group: the first group has mean mark

$$\frac{4 + 7 + 10}{3} = \frac{21}{3} = 7$$

The second group has mean mark

$$\frac{7 + 7 + 7}{3} = \frac{21}{3} = 7$$

We see that both groups have the same mean mark even though the marks in the first group are widely spread, whereas the marks in the second group are all the same. If the teacher quotes just the mean mark of each group this gives no information about how widely the marks are spread. The **variance** and **standard deviation** are important and widely used statistical quantities that contain this information. Most calculators are pre-programmed to calculate these quantities. Once you understand the processes involved, check to see if your calculator can be used to find the variance and standard deviation of a set of data.

Suppose we have n values x_1, x_2, x_3 up to x_n. Their mean is $\bar{x}$ given by

$$\bar{x} = \frac{\sum_{i=1}^{n} x_i}{n}$$

The variance is found from the following formula:

Key point

$$\text{variance} = \frac{\sum_{i=1}^{n} (x_i - \bar{x})^2}{n}$$

If you study this carefully you will see that to calculate the variance we must:

- calculate the mean value $\bar{x}$
- subtract the mean from each value in turn, that is find $x_i - \bar{x}$
- square each answer to get $(x_i - \bar{x})^2$
- add up all these squared quantities to get $\sum_{i=1}^{n} (x_i - \bar{x})^2$
- divide the result by n to get

$$\frac{\sum_{i=1}^{n} (x_i - \bar{x})^2}{n}$$

which is the variance

The standard deviation is found by taking the square root of the variance:

Key point

$$\text{standard deviation} = \sqrt{\frac{\sum_{i=1}^{n} (x_i - \bar{x})^2}{n}}$$

Let us calculate the variance and standard deviation of each of the two sets of marks 4, 7, 10 and 7, 7, 7. We have already noted that the mean of each set is 7. Each stage of the calculation of the variance of the set 4, 7, 10 is shown in Table 29.5. The mean is subtracted from each number, and the results are squared and then added. Note that when a negative number is squared the result is positive. The squares are added to give 18. In this

Table 29.5

x_i	$x_i - \bar{x}$	$(x_i - \bar{x})^2$
4	$4 - 7 = -3$	$(-3)^2 = 9$
7	$7 - 7 = 0$	$0^2 = 0$
10	$10 - 7 = 3$	$3^2 = 9$
Total		18

example, the number of values equals 3. So, taking $n = 3$,

$$\text{variance} = \frac{\sum_{i=1}^{n} (x_i - \bar{x})^2}{n} = \frac{18}{3} = 6$$

The standard deviation is the square root of the variance, that is $\sqrt{6} = 2.449$. Similarly, calculation of the variance and standard deviation of the set 7, 7, 7 is shown in Table 29.6. Again, n equals 3. So

$$\text{variance} = \frac{\sum_{i=1}^{n} (x_i - \bar{x})^2}{n} = \frac{0}{3} = 0$$

Table 29.6

x_i	$x_i - \bar{x}$	$(x_i - \bar{x})^2$
7	$7 - 7 = 0$	$0^2 = 0$
7	$7 - 7 = 0$	$0^2 = 0$
7	$7 - 7 = 0$	$0^2 = 0$
Total		0

The standard deviation is the square root of the variance and so it also equals zero. The fact that the standard deviation is zero reflects that there is no spread of values. By comparison it is easy to check that the standard deviation of the set 6, 7 and 8, which also has mean 7, is equal to 0.816. The fact that the set 4, 7 and 10 has standard deviation 2.449 shows that the values are more widely spread than in the set 6, 7 and 8.

WORKED EXAMPLE

29.11   Find the variance and standard deviation of 10, 15.8, 19.2 and 8.7.

Solution   First the mean is found:

$$\bar{x} = \frac{10 + 15.8 + 19.2 + 8.7}{4} = \frac{53.7}{4} = 13.425$$

The calculation to find the variance is given in Table 29.7.

$$\text{variance} = \frac{\sum_{i=1}^{n} (x_i - \bar{x})^2}{n} = \frac{73.049}{4} = 18.262$$

The standard deviation is the square root of the variance:

$$\sqrt{18.262} = 4.273$$

Table 29.7

x_i	$x_i - \bar{x}$	$(x_i - \bar{x})^2$
10	$10 - 13.425 = -3.425$	$(-3.425)^2 = 11.731$
15.8	$15.8 - 13.425 = 2.375$	$2.375^2 = 5.641$
19.2	$19.2 - 13.425 = 5.775$	$5.775^2 = 33.351$
8.7	$8.7 - 13.425 = -4.725$	$(-4.725)^2 = 22.326$
Total		73.049

When dealing with a grouped frequency distribution with N classes the formula for the variance becomes:

Key point

$$\text{variance} = \frac{\sum_{i=1}^{N} f_i(x_i - \bar{x})^2}{\sum_{i=1}^{N} f_i}$$

As before, the standard deviation is the square root of the variance.

WORKED EXAMPLE

29.12   In a period of 30 consecutive days in July the temperature in °C was recorded as follows:

18 19 20 23 24 24 21 18 17 16
16 17 17 17 18 19 20 20 22 23
24 24 25 23 21 21 20 19 19 18

(a) Produce a grouped frequency distribution showing data grouped from 16 to 17 °C, 18 to 19 °C and so on.
(b) Find the mean temperature of the grouped data.
(c) Find the standard deviation of the grouped data.

Solution   (a) The data is grouped using a tally chart as in Table 29.8.

Table 29.8

Temperature range (°C)	Tally	Frequency
16–17	ЖН̄ I	6
18–19	ЖН̄ III	8
20–21	ЖН̄ II	7
22–23	IIII	4
24–25	ЖН̄	5
Total		30

(b) When calculating the mean temperature from the grouped data we do not know the actual temperatures. We do know the frequency of each class. The best we can do is use the midpoint of each class as an estimate of the values in that class. The class midpoints and the calculation to determine the mean are shown in Table 29.9. The mean is then

$$\bar{x} = \frac{\sum_{i=1}^{N} f_i \times x_i}{\sum_{i=1}^{N} f_i} = \frac{603}{30} = 20.1 \ ^\circ C$$

Table 29.9

Temperature range (°C)	Frequency f_i	Class midpoint x_i	$f_i \times x_i$
16–17	6	16.5	99.0
18–19	8	18.5	148.0
20–21	7	20.5	143.5
22–23	4	22.5	90.0
24–25	5	24.5	122.5
Total	30		603

(c) To find the variance and hence the standard deviation we must subtract the mean, 20.1, from each value, square and then add the results. Finally this sum is divided by 30. The complete calculation is shown in Table 29.10.

Table 29.10

Temperature range (°C)	Frequency f_i	Class midpoint x_i	$x_i - \bar{x}$	$(x_i - \bar{x})^2$	$f_i(x_i - \bar{x})^2$
16–17	6	16.5	−3.60	12.96	77.76
18–19	8	18.5	−1.60	2.56	20.48
20–21	7	20.5	0.40	0.16	1.12
22–23	4	22.5	2.40	5.76	23.04
24–25	5	24.5	4.40	19.36	96.80
Total	30				219.20

Finally the variance is given by

$$\text{variance} = \frac{\sum_{i=1}^{N} f_i(x_i - \bar{x})^2}{\sum_{i=1}^{N} f_i} = \frac{219.20}{30} = 7.307$$

The standard deviation is the square root of the variance, that is $\sqrt{7.307} = 2.703$.

Self-assessment questions 29.3

1. Why is an average often an insufficient way of describing a set of values?

2. Describe the stages involved in calculating the variance and standard deviation of a set of values $x_1, x_2, \ldots, x_n$.

Exercise 29.3

MyMathLab

1. Find the standard deviation of each of the following sets of numbers and comment upon your answers:
   (a) 20, 20, 20, 20 (b) 16, 17, 23, 24
   (c) 0, 20, 20, 40

2. Calculate the variance and standard deviation of the following set of numbers: 1, 2, 3, 3, 3, 4, 7, 8, 9, 10.

3. The examination results of two students, Jane and Tony, are shown in the table. Find the mean and standard deviation of each of them. Comment upon the results.

	Jane	Tony
Maths	50	29
Physics	42	41
Chemistry	69	60
French	34	48
Spanish	62	80

4. The marks of 50 students in a mathematics examination are given as

45	50	62	62	68	47	45	44	48
73	62	63	62	67	80	45	41	40
23	55	21	83	67	49	48	48	62
63	79	58	71	37	32	58	54	50
62	66	68	62	81	92	62	45	49
71	72	70	49	51				

   (a) Produce a grouped frequency distribution using classes 25–29, 30–34, 35–39 and so on.
   (b) The modal class is the class with the highest frequency. State the modal class.
   (c) Calculate the mean, variance and standard deviation of the grouped frequency distribution.

Test and assignment exercises 29

1. Calculate the mean, median and mode of the following numbers: 2.7, 2.8, 3.1, 3.1, 3.1, 3.4, 3.8, 4.1.

2. Calculate the mean of
   (a) the first 10 whole numbers,

   $$1, 2, \ldots, 10$$

(b) the first 12 whole numbers,

$$1, 2, \ldots, 12$$

(c) the first n whole numbers,

$$1, 2, \ldots, n$$

3. A manufacturer of breakfast cereals uses two machines that pack 250 g packets of cereal automatically. In order to check the average weight, sample packets are taken and weighed to the nearest gram. The results of checking eight packets from each of the two machines are given in the table.

Machine

1	250	250	251	257	253	250	268	259
2	249	251	250	251	252	258	254	250

(a) Find the mean weight of each sample of eight packets.
(b) Find the standard deviation of each sample.
(c) Comment upon the performance of the two machines.

4. What is the median of the five numbers 18, 28, 39, 42, 43? If 50 is added as the sixth number what would the median become?

5. Express the following sums in sigma notation:

(a) $y_1 + y_2 + y_3 + \cdots + y_7 + y_8$
(b) $y_1^2 + y_2^2 + y_3^2 + \cdots + y_7^2 + y_8^2$
(c) $(y_1 - \bar{y})^2 + (y_2 - \bar{y})^2 + \cdots + (y_7 - \bar{y})^2 + (y_8 - \bar{y})^2$

Probability

Objectives: This chapter:

■ introduces theoretical and experimental probability and how to calculate them

■ explains the meaning of the term 'complementary events'

■ explains the meaning of the term 'independent events'

30.1 Introduction

Some events in life are impossible; other events are quite certain to happen. For example, it is impossible for a human being to live for 1000 years. We say that the probability of a human being living for 1000 years is 0. On the other hand it is quite certain that all of us will die someday. We say that the probability that all of us will die is 1. Using the letter P to stand for probability we can write

P(a human will live for 1000 years) $= 0$

and

P(all of us will die someday) $= 1$

Many other events in life are neither impossible nor certain. These have varying degrees of likelihood, or chance. For example, it is quite unlikely but not impossible that the British weather throughout a particular summer will be dominated by snowfall. It is quite likely but not certain that the life expectancy of the UK population will continue to rise in the foreseeable future. Events such as these can be assigned probabilities varying from 0 up to 1. Those having probabilities close to 1 are quite likely to happen. Those having probabilities close to 0 are almost impossible. Several events and their probabilities are shown on the

Figure 30.1
The probability scale

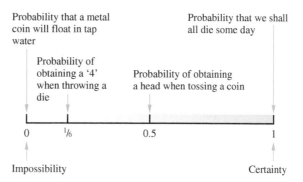

probability scale in Figure 30.1. It is important to note that no probability can lie outside the range 0 to 1.

All probabilities lie in the range [0, 1].

Complementary events

Consider the following situation. A light bulb is tested. Clearly it either works or it does not work. Here we have two events: the first is that the light bulb works and the second is that the light bulb does not work. When the bulb is tested, one or other of these events must occur. Furthermore, each event excludes the other. In such a situation we say the two events are **complementary**. In general, two events are complementary if one of them must happen and, when it does, the other event cannot. The sum of the probabilities of the two complementary events must always equal 1. This is known as **total probability**. We shall see how this result can be used to calculate probabilities shortly.

Self-assessment questions 30.1

1. All probabilities must lie in a certain range. What is this range?

2. Explain the meaning of the term 'complementary events'.

30.2   Calculating theoretical probabilities

Sometimes we have sufficient information about a set of circumstances to calculate the probability of an event occurring. For example, suppose we roll a die and ask what the probability is of obtaining a score of '5'. If the die is fair, or **unbiased**, the chance of getting a '5' is the same as the chance of getting any other score. You would expect to get a '5' one time in every six. That is,

the probability of throwing a '5' is $\dfrac{1}{6}$ or 0.167

In other words there is a one in six chance of scoring a '5'. The fact that the probability is closer to 0 than to 1 means that it is quite unlikely that a '5' will be thrown, although it is not impossible. Such a probability is known as a **theoretical probability** and, when all events are equally likely, it is calculated from the following formula:

Key point

When all events are equally likely

$$P\left(\begin{array}{c}\text{obtaining our} \\ \text{chosen event}\end{array}\right) = \dfrac{\text{number of ways the chosen event can occur}}{\text{total number of possibilities}}$$

For example, suppose we ask what the probability is of obtaining a score more than 4. A score more than 4 can occur in two ways, by scoring a '5' or a '6'. If the die is fair, all possible events are equally likely. The total number of possibilities is 6, therefore,

$$P(\text{score more than 4}) = \dfrac{2}{6} = \dfrac{1}{3}$$

WORKED EXAMPLES

30.1   A fair die is thrown. What is the probability of obtaining an even score?

Solution   The chosen event is throwing an even score, that is a '2', '4' or '6'. There are therefore three ways that this chosen event can occur out of a total of six, equally likely, ways. So

$$P(\text{even score}) = \dfrac{3}{6} = \dfrac{1}{2}$$

30.2   A fair coin is tossed. What is the probability that it will land with its head uppermost?

Solution   There are two equally likely ways the coin can land: head uppermost or tail uppermost. The chosen event, that the coin lands with its head uppermost, is just one of these ways. The chance of getting a head is the same as the chance of getting a tail. Therefore,

$$P(\text{head}) = \dfrac{1}{2}$$

Note from the previous example that $P(\text{tail}) = \frac{1}{2}$ and that also

$P(\text{tail}) + P(\text{head}) = 1$

Note that the two events, getting a head and getting a tail, are complementary because one of them must happen and either one excludes the other. Therefore the sum of the two probabilities, the total probability, equals 1.

WORKED EXAMPLE

30.3   Two coins are tossed.

(a) Write down all the possible outcomes.

(b) What is the probability of obtaining two tails?

Solution   (a) Letting H stand for head and T for tail, the possible outcomes are

H, H H, T T, H T, T

There are four possible outcomes, each one equally likely to occur.

(b) Obtaining two tails is just one of the four possible outcomes. Therefore, the probability of obtaining two tails is $\frac{1}{4}$.

Exercise 30.2

1. A die is thrown. Find
    (a) the probability of obtaining a score less than 6
    (b) the probability of obtaining a score more than 6
    (c) the probability of obtaining an even score less than 5
    (d) the probability of obtaining an even score less than 2

2. There are four Aces in a pack of 52 playing cards. What is the probability that a card selected at random is not an Ace?

3. A drawer contains six red socks, six black socks and eight blue socks. Find the probability that a sock selected at random from the drawer is
    (a) black   (b) red   (c) red or blue

4. Two dice are thrown together and their scores are added together. By considering all the possible outcomes, find the probability that the total score will be
    (a) 12   (b) 0   (c) 1   (d) 2   (e) more than 5

5. A basket contains 87 good apples and three bad ones. What is the probability that an apple chosen at random is bad?

6. A box contains 16 red blocks, 20 blue blocks, 24 orange blocks and 10 black blocks. A block is picked at random. Calculate the probability that the block is
    (a) black   (b) orange   (c) blue
    (d) red or blue   (e) red or blue or orange
    (f) not orange

7. Three coins are tossed. By considering all possible outcomes calculate the probability of obtaining
    (a) two heads and one tail
    (b) at least two heads
    (c) no heads

30.3 Calculating experimental probabilities

In some circumstances we do not have sufficient information to calculate a theoretical probability. We know that if a coin is unbiased the probability of obtaining a head is $\frac{1}{2}$. But suppose the coin is biased so that it is more likely to land with its tail uppermost. We can experiment by tossing the coin a large number of times and counting the number of tails obtained. Suppose we toss the coin 100 times and obtain 65 tails. We can then estimate the probability of obtaining a tail as $\frac{65}{100}$ or 0.65. Such a probability is known as an **experimental probability** and is accurate only if a very large number of experiments are performed. Generally, we can calculate an experimental probability from the following formula:

Key point

$$P\left(\begin{array}{c}\text{chosen event} \\ \text{occurs}\end{array}\right) = \frac{\text{number of ways the chosen event occurs}}{\text{total number of times the experiment is repeated}}$$

WORKED EXAMPLES

30.4   A biased die is thrown 1000 times and a score of '6' is obtained on 200 occasions. If the die is now thrown again what is the probability of obtaining a score of '6'?

Solution   Using the formula for the experimental probability we find

$$P(\text{throwing a '6'}) = \frac{200}{1000} = 0.2$$

If the die were unbiased the theoretical probability of throwing a '6' would be $\frac{1}{6} = 0.167$, so the die has been biased in favour of throwing a '6'.

30.5   A manufacturer produces microwave ovens. It is known from experience that the probability that a microwave oven is of an acceptable standard is 0.92. Find the probability that an oven selected at random is not of an acceptable standard.

Solution   When an oven is tested either it is of an acceptable standard or it is not. An oven cannot be both acceptable and unacceptable. The two events, that the oven is acceptable or that the oven is unacceptable, are therefore complementary. Recall that the sum of the probabilities of complementary events is 1 and so

$$P(\text{oven is not acceptable}) = 1 - 0.92 = 0.08$$

Self-assessment questions 30.3

1. In what circumstances is it appropriate to use an experimental probability?

2. A series of experiments is performed three times. In the first of the series an experiment is carried out 100 times. In the second it is carried out 1000 times and in the third 10000 times. Which of the series of experiments is likely to lead to the best estimate of probability? Why?

Exercise 30.3

1. A new component is fitted to a washing machine. In a sample of 150 machines tested, 7 failed to function correctly. Calculate the probability that a machine fitted with the new component (a) works correctly, (b) does not work correctly.

2. In a sample containing 5000 nails manufactured by a company, 5% are too short or too long. A nail is picked at random from the production line. Estimate the probability that it is of the right length.

3. The probability that the Post Office delivers first-class mail on the following working day after posting is 0.96. If 93500 first-class letters are posted on Wednesday, how many are likely to be delivered on Thursday?

4. The probability that a car rescue service will reach a car in less than one hour is 0.87. If the rescue service is called out 17300 times in one day, calculate the number of cars reached in less than one hour.

5. Out of 50000 components tested, 48700 were found to be working well. A batch of 3000 components is delivered to a depot. How many are likely to be not working well?

30.4   Independent events

Two events are **independent** if the occurrence of either one in no way affects the occurrence of the other. For example, if an unbiased die is thrown twice the score on the second throw is in no way affected by the score on the first. The two scores are independent. The **multiplication law** for independent events states the following:

Key point   If events A and B are independent, then the probability of obtaining A and B is given by

$$P(A \text{ and } B) = P(A) \times P(B)$$

WORKED EXAMPLE

30.6   A die is thrown and a coin is tossed. What is the probability of obtaining a '6' and a head?

Solution   These events are independent since the score on the die in no way affects the result of tossing the coin, and vice versa. Therefore

$$P(\text{throwing a '6' and tossing a head}) = P(\text{throwing a '6'})$$
$$\times P(\text{tossing a head})$$
$$= \frac{1}{6} \times \frac{1}{2}$$
$$= \frac{1}{12}$$

When several events are independent of each other the multiplication law becomes

$$P(A \text{ and } B \text{ and } C \text{ and } D \ldots) = P(A) \times P(B) \times P(C) \times P(D) \ldots$$

WORKED EXAMPLE

30.7   A coin is tossed three times. What is the probability of obtaining three heads?

Solution   The three tosses are all independent events since the result of any one has no effect on the others. Therefore

$$P(3 \text{ heads}) = \frac{1}{2} \times \frac{1}{2} \times \frac{1}{2} = \frac{1}{8}$$

Self-assessment questions 30.4

1. Explain what is meant by saying two events are independent.

2. Suppose we have two packs each of 52 playing cards. A card is selected from each pack. Event A is that the card from the first pack is the Ace of Spades. Event B is that the card from the second pack is a Spade. Are these two events dependent or independent?

3. From a single pack of cards, two are removed. The first is examined. Suppose event A is that the first card is the Ace of Spades. The second card is examined. Event B is that the second card is a Spade. Are the two events dependent or independent?

Exercise 30.4

1. A die is thrown and a coin is tossed. What is the probability of getting an even score on the die and a tail?

2. Suppose you have two packs each of 52 playing cards. A card is drawn from the first and a card is drawn from the second. What is the probability that both cards are the Ace of Spades?

3. A coin is tossed eight times. What is the probability of obtaining eight tails?

4. A die is thrown four times. What is the probability of obtaining four '1's?

5. Suppose that there is an equal chance of a mother giving birth to a boy or a girl.
   (a) If one child is born find the probability that it is a boy.

   (b) If two children are born find the probability that they are both boys, assuming that the sex of neither one can influence the sex of the other.

6. The probability that a component is working well is 0.96. If four components are picked at random calculate the probability that
   (a) they all work well
   (b) none of them work well

7. The probability that a student passes a module is 0.91. If three modules are studied calculate the probability that the student passes
   (a) all three modules   (b) two modules
   (b) one module   (d) no modules

Test and assignment exercises 30

1. The following numbers are probabilities of a certain event happening. One of them is an error. Which one?
   (a) 0.5   (b) $\dfrac{3}{4}$ (c) 0.001   (d) $\dfrac{13}{4}$

2. Which of the following cannot be a probability?
   (a) 0.125   (b) −0.2   (c) 1   (d) 0

3. Events A, B and C are defined as follows. In each case state the complementary event.
   A: the lifespan of a light bulb is greater than 1000 hours
   B: it will rain on Christmas Day 2020
   C: your car will be stolen sometime in the next 100 days

4. The probability of a component manufactured in a factory being defective is 0.01. If three components are selected at random what is the probability that they all work as required?

5. A parcel delivery company guarantees 'next-day' delivery for 99% of its parcels. Out of a sample of 1800 deliveries, 15 were delivered later than the following day. Is the company living up to its promises?

6. At a certain bus stop the probability of a bus arriving late is $\frac{3}{20}$. The probability of its arriving on time is $\frac{4}{5}$. Find
   (a) the probability that the bus arrives early
   (b) the probability that the bus does not arrive late

7. Suppose you have two packs each of 52 playing cards. A card is drawn from the first and a card is drawn from the second. What is the probability that
   (a) both cards are diamonds?
   (b) both cards are black?
   (c) both cards are Kings?

8. Find the probability of obtaining an odd number when throwing a fair die once.

9. A bag contains eight red beads, four white beads and five blue beads. A bead is drawn at random. Determine the probability that it is
   (a) red   (b) white   (c) black   (d) blue   (e) red or white   (f) not blue

10. Two cards are selected from a pack of 52. Find the probability that they are both Aces if the first card is
    (a) replaced and   (b) not replaced

11. A pack contains 20 cards, numbered 1 to 20. A card is picked at random. Calculate the probability that the number on the card is
    (a) even   (b) 16 or more   (c) divisible by 3

12. Out of 42300 components, 846 were defective. How many defective components would you expect in a batch of 1500?

13. A biased die has the following probabilities:
    $P(1) = 0.1$, $P(2) = 0.15$, $P(3) = 0.1$,

    $P(4) = 0.2$, $P(5) = 0.2$, $P(6) = 0.25$

    The die is thrown twice. Calculate the probability that
    (a) both scores are '6's
    (b) both scores are '1's
    (c) the first score is odd and the second is even
    (d) the total score is 10

Correlation

Objectives: This chapter:

- explains how to explore the association between two variables using a scatter diagram.
- explains what is meant by positive, negative and zero correlation
- introduces the product-moment correlation coefficient
- introduces Spearman's coefficient of rank correlation

31.1 Introduction

In the sciences, business, health studies, geography, and many other fields, we are often interested in exploring relationships that may exist between two variables. For example, might it be true that, in general, taller people have greater weight than shorter people? Do cars with larger engine sizes travel fewer miles using a gallon of petrol than those with smaller engine sizes? Do business studies students who are good at statistics perform well in another aspect of their course?

The answers to some of these questions can be obtained using the statistics of **correlation**. As a first step, a graphical representation of the data is prepared using a **scatter diagram**. This is a simple method which helps us quickly draw some conclusions about the data. When a more quantitative, or rigorous, approach is needed a quantity known as the **correlation coefficient** can be calculated. This associates a number with the relationship between the variables and enables us to describe the strength of the relationship, or correlation, as perfect, strong, weak, or non-existent. Under certain conditions we may be able to predict the value of one variable from knowledge of the other.

This chapter explains how to draw and interpret a scatter diagram, and how to calculate two types of correlation coefficient: the product-moment correlation coefficient, and Spearman's coefficient of rank correlation. Chapter 32 explains how we can use a technique known as **regression** to predict values of one variable when we know values of the other.

31.2 Scatter diagrams

A simple and practical way of exploring relationships between two variables is the scatter diagram. Consider the following worked example.

WORKED EXAMPLE

31.1   In a study of food production in a developing country the total crop of wheat (in units of 10000 tonnes) was measured over a period of five summers. The summer rainfall (in cm) was also recorded. The data is provided in Table 31.1. Use a scatter diagram to explore the relationship between rainfall and wheat crop.

Table 31.1

Year	1	2	3	4	5
Wheat crop (10000 tonnes)	42	38	48	51	45
Rainfall (cm)	20	19	30	34	24

To draw a scatter diagram we think of each data pair (that is, each pair of values of rainfall and wheat crop, such as 20 and 42) as the coordinates of a point.

We choose one of the variables to be plotted on the horizontal axis and one on the vertical axis. At this stage, when we are simply exploring whether a relationship may exist, it does not matter which. In Figure 31.1

Figure 31.1
Scatter diagram showing the association between rainfall and wheat crop

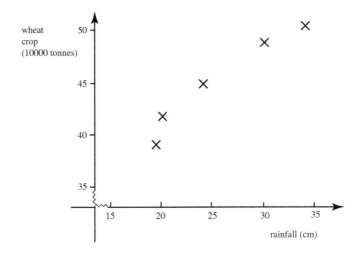

rainfall has been plotted on the horizonal axis and wheat crop on the vertical. Each point is represented by a ×.

The scatter diagram in Figure 31.1 shows that the points appear to cluster around an imaginary line which slopes upwards from left to right. There appears to be a **linear relationship** between the two variables.

The line around which the points cluster has been drawn in by eye in Figure 31.2, although this line is not part of the scatter diagram. This line, which is closest, in some sense, to all of the data points, is called **the line of best fit**. We shall see in Chapter 32 how the equation of this line can be calculated exactly. Note that this line has a positive slope, or gradient. (You may find it useful to refresh your knowledge by re-reading Chapter 18.) When the points cluster closely around a line with a positive gradient we are observing **strong positive correlation** between the two variables.

Figure 31.2
The scatter diagram of Worked Example 31.1 showing the line of best fit

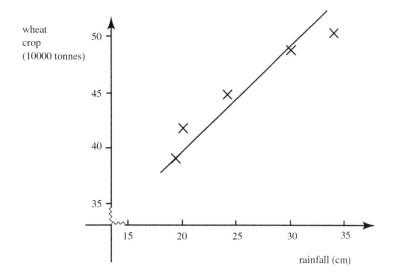

The scatter diagram suggests that there is indeed a strong (linear) relationship between the two variables with low wheat crop being associated with low rainfall and high wheat crop associated with high rainfall.

Scatter diagrams can take different forms. For example, the one in Figure 31.3(a) shows that the points cluster around a line with positive gradient but not so closely as in Figure 31.2. This is an example of weak, but positive correlation. There appears to be a relationship between the two variables but this is not as strong as in Figure 31.2.

Figure 31.3(b) shows that the points cluster closely around a line with a negative gradient. The variables here exhibit strong negative correlation. This means that high values of one variable are associated with low values of the other, and vice versa. In Figure 31.3(c) there is weak negative correlation. Finally, in Figure 31.3(d) the points do not lie on or close to a straight line at all. These points exhibit no correlation whatsoever.

When all points lie exactly on a straight line, whether with positive or negative gradient, the correlation is said to be perfect.

Key point

If X and Y are positively correlated then, on the whole, as X increases, Y increases.

If X and Y are negatively correlated then, on the whole, as X increases, Y decreases.

Figure 31.3
Scatter diagrams can illustrate different forms of association

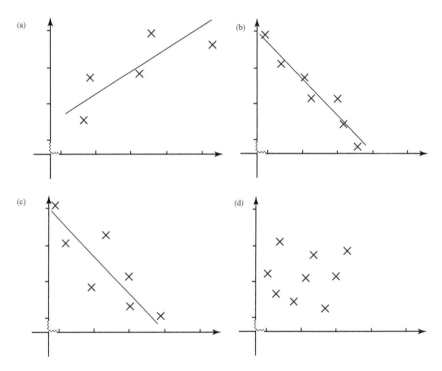

It is also possible that a relationship exists between two variables but that this relationship is not of a linear nature. For example, the scatter diagram in Figure 31.4 seems to indicate that the points lie on a well defined curve, but not on a straight line. Statistical techniques to explore non-linear relationships such as this are available but are beyond the scope of this book.

Figure 31.4
A non-linear association
between two variables

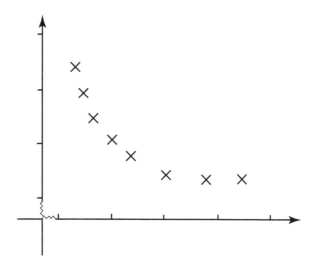

Self-assessment questions 31.2

1. Explain the purpose of a scatter diagram.

2. Explain what is meant by positive correlation, negative correlation and zero correlation.

3. Give an example of your own of two variables which might be positively correlated.

4. Give an example of your own of two variables which might be negatively correlated.

Exercise 31.2

1. For each of the following sets of data plot a scatter diagram. If possible, draw conclusions about the nature of a possible relationship between the two variables.
   (a)

X	2	8	5	4	10
Y	9	6	8	7	4

   (b)

X	50	52	54	56	58	60
Y	42	48	36	50	37	46

2. A Human Resources department in a company gathers data on the age (in years) and salary (in £1000's) of a particular group of employees. The data is given in the table on the next page. Draw a scatter diagram for this data and comment upon the nature of the relationship between age and salary.

age	18	19	19	28	35	36	49	50	50
salary	12	13	14	18	20	21	30	38	21

31.3 Correlation coefficient

As we have seen, a scatter diagram can give us useful graphical information about the relationship between two variables. But when we require a more precise measure of a relationship, a useful quantity is the **correlation coefficient**, denoted by r. This is a number which measures the strength of the correlation. It lies between -1 and $+1$. When r takes the value 1 there is an exact straight line relationship with a positive gradient, and thus perfect positive correlation. When it takes the value -1 there is also a straight line relationship, but this time with a negative gradient. This is perfect negative correlation. When the value of r is 0 there is no correlation whatsoever. When r is close to 1 we have strong positive correlation. When r is close to -1 there is strong negative correlation.

Suppose we have gathered data in the form of n pairs of values of quantities X and Y. Suppose we denote the values of X by x_i and the values of Y by y_i where i takes values $1 \ldots n$. We can write the n pairs of values in the form (x_i, y_i). The **product-moment correlation coefficient**, r, is given by

$$r = \frac{\sum_{i=1}^{n}(x_i - \bar{x})(y_i - \bar{y})}{\sqrt{\sum_{i=1}^{n}(x_i - \bar{x})^2 \sum_{i=1}^{n}(y_i - \bar{y})^2}}$$

where $\bar{x}$ is the mean of the x values, and $\bar{y}$ is the mean of the y values. In practice, when calculating the correlation coefficient by hand some regard it as easier to work with an alternative, but equivalent, version of the formula. This version avoids prior calculation of the mean values of x and y and also the differences from the mean values. It states

$$r = \frac{n\sum_{i=1}^{n}x_i y_i - \sum_{i=1}^{n}x_i \sum_{i=1}^{n}y_i}{\sqrt{n\sum_{i=1}^{n}x_i^2 - \left(\sum_{i=1}^{n}x_i\right)^2}\sqrt{n\sum_{i=1}^{n}y_i^2 - \left(\sum_{i=1}^{n}y_i\right)^2}}$$

We shall provide examples illustrating both versions.

Key point

When we have n pairs of values (x_i, y_i) of two variables X and Y, the product-moment correlation coefficient, r, is given either by

$$r = \frac{\sum_{i=1}^{n}(x_i - \bar{x})(y_i - \bar{y})}{\sqrt{\sum_{i=1}^{n}(x_i - \bar{x})^2 \sum_{i=1}^{n}(y_i - \bar{y})^2}}$$

or, equivalently, by

$$r = \frac{n\sum_{i=1}^{n}x_i y_i - \sum_{i=1}^{n}x_i \sum_{i=1}^{n}y_i}{\sqrt{n\sum_{i=1}^{n}x_i^2 - \left(\sum_{i=1}^{n}x_i\right)^2}\sqrt{n\sum_{i=1}^{n}y_i^2 - \left(\sum_{i=1}^{n}y_i\right)^2}}$$

If $r = 0$ there is no correlation.
If $0 < r \leq 1$ there is positive correlation.
If $-1 \leq r < 0$ there is negative correlation.
If r is close to 1 or -1 the correlation is strong.
If r is close to 0 the correlation is weak.

These formulae seem daunting, especially when first met. Work through the following example to see how to use them to calculate a correlation coefficient. In practice, once you understand what is going on you will be able to use a computer package such as Excel which has built-in commands for performing such calculations.

WORKED EXAMPLES

31.2 Four pairs of observations (x_i, y_i) of two quantities, X and Y, are listed in Table 31.2. To explore a possible relationship between the values of X and Y calculate the correlation coefficient, r, using the first of the given formulae.

Table 31.2

x_i	y_i
9	20
21	42
33	61
45	79

To calculate r it is first necessary to find the mean of the four x values, $\bar{x}$, and the mean of the four y values, $\bar{y}$. These calculations are shown in Table 31.3.

Table 31.3

x_i	y_i
9	20
21	42
33	61
45	79
108	202

$$\bar{x} = \tfrac{108}{4} = 27 \quad \bar{y} = \tfrac{202}{4} = 50.5$$

Then $\bar{x}$ is subtracted from each x value and $\bar{y}$ is subtracted from each y value, before various products are found. This information is best presented in a table, such as that in Table 31.4.

Table 31.4

x_i	y_i	$x_i - \bar{x}$	$y_i - \bar{y}$	$(x_i - \bar{x})(y_i - \bar{y})$	$(x_i - \bar{x})^2$	$(y_i - \bar{y})^2$
9	20	-18	-30.5	549	324	930.25
21	42	-6	-8.5	51	36	72.25
33	61	6	10.5	63	36	110.25
45	79	18	28.5	513	324	812.25
$\bar{x} = 27$	$\bar{y} = 50.5$	0	0	1176	720	1925

With the table complete all the quantities required in the formula for r are available:

$$r = \frac{\sum_{i=1}^{n}(x_i - \bar{x})(y_i - \bar{y})}{\sqrt{\sum_{i=1}^{n}(x_i - \bar{x})^2 \sum_{i=1}^{n}(y_i - \bar{y})^2}} = \frac{1176}{\sqrt{(720)(1925)}} = 0.9989$$

With a value of r so close to $+1$ we conclude that there is very strong positive correlation between the variables x and y.

31.3 For the data in Worked Example 31.2 recalculate r using the second of the formulae to confirm that the result is the same.

Solution   As before, we draw up a table showing the quantities required (Table 31.5):

x_i	y_i	x_i^2	y_i^2	x_iy_i
9	20	81	400	180
21	42	441	1764	882
33	61	1089	3721	2013
45	79	2025	6241	3555
108	202	3636	12126	6630

This data can be substituted into the formula:

$$r = \frac{n\sum_{i=1}^{n} x_i y_i - \sum_{i=1}^{n} x_i \sum_{i=1}^{n} y_i}{\sqrt{n\sum_{i=1}^{n} x_i^2 - \left(\sum_{i=1}^{n} x_i\right)^2}\sqrt{n\sum_{i=1}^{n} y_i^2 - \left(\sum_{i=1}^{n} y_i\right)^2}}$$

$$= \frac{4(6630) - (108)(202)}{\sqrt{4(3636) - 108^2}\sqrt{4(12126) - 202^2}}$$

$$= \frac{4704}{\sqrt{2880}\sqrt{7700}}$$

$$= 0.9989 \quad \text{to 4 d.p.}$$

This confirms the same result is obtained using either version of the formulae.

31.4   In a recent survey of new cars data was collected on the engine size (in cubic centimetres (cc)) and the fuel economy measured in miles per gallon (mpg). The fuel economy is calculated by simulating driving in both urban and extra-urban conditions. The data is presented in Table 31.6. Calculate the correlation coefficient for this data and comment upon the answer.

$x =$ engine size (cc)	$y =$ economy (mpg)
999	57.6
1498	45.6
1596	37.7
1998	38.2
2295	28.8
6750	13.7

First we calculate the mean of the x and y values as shown in Table 31.7.

Table 31.7

x = engine size (cc)	y = economy (mpg)
999	57.6
1498	45.6
1596	37.7
1998	38.2
2295	28.8
6750	13.7

$$\bar{x} = \frac{15136}{6} = 2522.7 \quad \bar{y} = \frac{221.6}{6} = 36.9$$

Then $\bar{x}$ is subtracted from each x value and $\bar{y}$ is subtracted from each y value, before various products are found. This information is best presented in a table, such as that in Table 31.8.

Table 31.8

x	y	$x_i - \bar{x}$	$y_i - \bar{y}$	$(x_i-\bar{x})(y_i-\bar{y})$	$(x_i-\bar{x})^2$	$(y_i-\bar{y})^2$
999	57.6	−1523.7	20.7	−31540.59	2321661.69	428.49
1498	45.6	−1024.7	8.7	−8914.89	1050010.09	75.69
1596	37.7	−926.7	0.8	−741.36	858772.89	0.64
1998	38.2	−524.7	1.3	−682.11	275310.09	1.69
2295	28.8	−227.7	−8.1	1844.37	51847.29	65.61
6750	13.7	4227.3	−23.2	−98073.36	17870065.29	538.24

$\bar{x} = 2522.7 \quad \bar{y} = 36.9$ $\qquad\qquad$ −138107.94 $\quad$ 22427667.34 $\quad$ 1110.36

With the table complete all the quantities required in the formula for r can be found:

$$r = \frac{\sum_{i=1}^{n}(x_i - \bar{x})(y_i - \bar{y})}{\sqrt{\sum_{i=1}^{n}(x_i - \bar{x})^2 \sum_{i=1}^{n}(y_i - \bar{y})^2}} = \frac{-138107.94}{\sqrt{(22427667.34)(1110.36)}} = -0.8752 \ (4 \text{d.p.})$$

With a value of r so close to −1 we conclude that there is very strong negative correlation between the variables x and y. This means that, on the basis of the data supplied here, there is strong negative correlation between engine size and fuel economy. In general, smaller-sized engines in our sample are more economical than the larger engines.

You should rework this example using the second of the formulae for r.

Self-assessment question 31.3

1. Describe in words the extent of association between two variables when (a) $r=1$, (b) $r=-0.82$, (c) $r=-0.33$, (d) $r=0$.

Exercise 31.3

1. Calculate the correlation coefficient r for the following data. Interpret your result.

x_i	y_i
1	11
3	51
4	96
5	115

2. Calculate the correlation coefficient r for the following data. Interpret your result.

x_i	y_i
0	2
1	5
2	8
3	11

3. Investigate the availability of computer software for the calculation of the correlation coefficient. Calculate the correlation coefficient for the data of Exercise 31.2, Question 2.

31.4 Spearman's coefficient of rank correlation

Sometimes specific values of two variables, X and Y say, are not available, but we may have data on their order, or **rank**. For example, suppose we have data on seven students, A, B, ..., F, G, which tells us who came first, second etc., in each of two athletic events – swimming and running. The data would take the form given in Table 31.9. So, for example, student A came first in both events, whereas student G came last in the swimming event and second from last in the running event.

Table 31.9

student	swimming rank	running rank
A	1	1
B	3	7
C	6	5
D	2	3
E	4	2
F	5	4
G	7	6

Suppose we want to know whether there is correlation between the two. Is there an association between good performance in the running event and good performance when swimming?

Spearman's formula can be used to calculate a **coefficient of rank correlation**, which is a number lying between −1 and 1 which provides information on the strength of the relationship exhibited by the data.

To apply the formula we need to find, for each pair of rank values, the **difference** between the ranks. So for student A, the difference between the ranks is $1 - 1 = 0$. For student G the difference is $7 - 6 = 1$. We do this for all pairs of values. Then each difference is squared. The detail is shown in Table 31.10.

Table 31.10

student	swimming rank	running rank	difference D	D^2
A	1	1	0	0
B	3	7	−4	16
C	6	5	1	1
D	2	3	−1	1
E	4	2	2	4
F	5	4	1	1
G	7	6	1	1

24

If there are n pairs of values, the coefficient of rank correlation is given by

$$r = 1 - \frac{6\sum_{i=1}^{n} D^2}{n(n^2 - 1)}$$

In this case $n = 7$ and so

$$r = 1 - \frac{6 \times 24}{7(7^2 - 1)} = 1 - \frac{144}{(7)(48)} = 0.57 \quad \text{(2 d.p.)}$$

On the basis of this data we can conclude there is a moderate positive correlation between performance in the two athletic events.

Key point

Spearman's coefficient of rank correlation: Given n pairs of values which are the rank orders of two variables X and Y, the **coefficient of rank correlation** is given by

$$r = 1 - \frac{6\sum_{i=1}^{n} D^2}{n(n^2 - 1)}$$

where D is the difference between the ranks of the corresponding values of X and Y.

Self assessment question 31.4

1. In what circumstances might you use the coefficient of rank correlation rather than the product-moment correlation coefficient?

Exercise 31.4

1. The table shows the rank order of six students in their mathematics and their science tests:

student	maths rank	science rank
A	1	1
B	3	6
C	6	5
D	2	3
E	4	2
F	5	4

Find the coefficient of rank correlation and comment upon the strength of any relationship.

2. The table shows the rank order of 10 countries in terms of the amount per capita spent upon education and the wealth of that country:

country	education spend per capita	wealth
A	4	6
B	3	4
C	6	5
D	5	7
E	7	8
F	8	9
G	10	10
H	9	1
I	1	3
J	2	2

Find the coefficient of rank correlation and comment upon the strength of any relationship.

3. Suppose you are given the rank orders of two variables and suppose that the ranks agree exactly: that is, when the rank of X is 1, the rank of Y is 1, and so on. Show that Spearman's coefficient of rank correlation, r, is 1. Further, show that when one ranking is the exact reverse of the other, the value of r is -1.

Test and assignment exercises 31

1. Calculate the correlation coefficient r for the following data. Interpret your result.

x_i	y_i
0	11
1	7
2	3

2. Figure 31.5 shows several scatter diagrams. Comment upon the nature of possible relationships between the two variables.

Figure 31.5

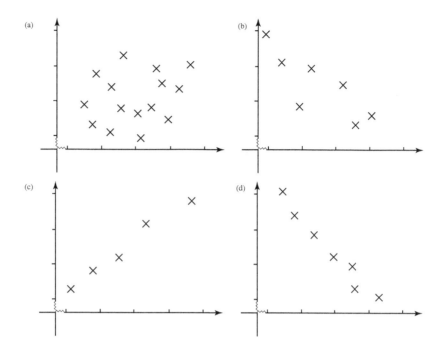

3. The table gives the mean summer temperature (in °C) at a holiday resort during the past six years together with volume (in litres) of ice cream purchased from local shops and vendors:

Year	1	2	3	4	5	6
Mean temperature (°C)	10	14	18	11	12	10
Volume (1000 litres)	20	32	33	24	23	18

Calculate the correlation coefficient for this data and comment upon any possible relationship.

4. The table provides data on seven families. It shows annual income and the amount spent in 2004 on family holidays. Rank the data and calculate Spearman's coefficient of rank correlation. Comment upon the calculated value.

family	annual income	holiday spend
A	24,000	875
B	56,000	5400
C	36,000	2100
D	29,500	400
E	100,000	1250
F	58,000	4250
G	38,000	2259

Regression

Objectives: This chapter:

- explains the concept of simple linear regression

- shows how to calculate the regression line of Y on X

- shows how to use the regression equation to predict values of the dependent variable, Y, given values of the independent variable, X

32.1 Introduction

In Chapter 31 we introduced **correlation** in order to explore the relationship between two variables, X and Y say, measured on some object of interest. We drew scatter diagrams to explore possible relationships visually and calculated the correlation coefficient, which gave us an indication of the strength of the relationship between the two variables.

In correlation, the two variables, X and Y, have equal 'status' and when a scatter diagram is drawn it does not matter which variable is plotted on the horizontal axis and which is plotted on the vertical axis. Whilst the diagrams will differ if we switch axes, the correlation coefficient will be the same either way. This is because it measures the degree of association between the two variables but does not attribute any dependency, cause or effect.

We now move on to study **regression**. The purpose of regression is to predict the value of one of the variables given a value of the other variable. When we use the data to predict the value of Y corresponding to a value of X that we choose, we refer to this as 'regression of Y on X'. So regression is subtly different from correlation. The status of the two variables is not the same since we are regarding Y as being a variable whose value depends upon the value we choose for X. In such cases we refer to X as the **independent variable**, and Y as the **dependent variable**. Statistical textbooks often refer to X as the **predictor** and Y as the **response variable** because from a value of X we can *predict* the corresponding value of Y.

For example, we might be interested in trying to predict the blood pressure of a member of a group of workers given his or her age. To do this we could select several members of the group, chosen by age, X, and measure their blood pressure, Y. We then use this data to calculate the regression of blood pressure on age. This produces a regression equation which can then predict the blood pressure (without actually measuring it) of another worker given only his or her age.

In any regression analysis, values of the independent variable, X, should be preselected. For example, we may decide to select workers aged 20, 25, 30, 35, 40, ..., 60 and measure the blood pressures, Y, of these chosen individuals. A scatter diagram is then drawn. Provided the diagram indicates that the points are scattered around an imaginary straight line then it is appropriate to calculate a **regression equation** for this line. This is the equation of the line which best fits the data and which can then be used to predict unknown values of Y.

32.2 The regression equation

Suppose we have gathered a set of data by selecting values of the variable, X, and measuring values of the corresponding variable, Y, upon each of n objects. Let the values of X be $x_1, x_2, \ldots, x_n$ and the corresponding values of Y be $y_1, y_2, \ldots, y_n$.

The regression equation is the equation of the straight line which most closely fits all of the given data. It is given in the standard form of an equation of a straight line which we shall write as

$$y = a + bx$$

(You may find it helpful to re-read Chapter 18.) So here, a is the vertical intercept of the line with the y axis, and b is the gradient of the line. The value of b is calculated first using the formula

$$b = \frac{n \sum_{i=1}^{n} x_i y_i - \left(\sum_{i=1}^{n} x_i \right) \left(\sum_{i=1}^{n} y_i \right)}{n \sum_{i=1}^{n} x_i^2 - \left(\sum_{i=1}^{n} x_i \right)^2}$$

The vertical intercept, a, is then given by

$$a = \frac{\sum_{i=1}^{n} y_i - b \sum_{i=1}^{n} x_i}{n}$$

The derivation of these formulae, which is beyond the scope of this book, relies on a technique which, loosely, makes the square of the vertical difference between each point on the scatter diagram and the line of best fit as small as possible. The proof can be found in most statistical textbooks. The formulae look very complicated when met for the first time, but in essence they require us simply to multiply some values together and add them up, as we shall see.

Key point

Given values of variables X and Y measured on n objects of interest, the regression line of Y on X is given by $y = a + bx$ where

$$b = \frac{n \sum_{i=1}^{n} x_i y_i - \left(\sum_{i=1}^{n} x_i \right) \left(\sum_{i=1}^{n} y_i \right)}{n \sum_{i=1}^{n} x_i^2 - \left(\sum_{i=1}^{n} x_i \right)^2} \qquad a = \frac{\sum_{i=1}^{n} y_i - b \sum_{i=1}^{n} x_i}{n}$$

WORKED EXAMPLE

32.1   Table 32.1 shows values of X and Y measured on five individuals.

Table 32.1

individual	x_i	y_i
A	10	28
B	20	32
C	30	38
D	40	39
E	50	48

(a) Use a scatter diagram to show that there appears to be a linear relationship between X and Y.
(b) Find the equation which represents the regression of Y on X.
(c) Plot the regression line on the scatter diagram.
(d) Use the equation to predict the value of Y when $X = 37$.

Solution   (a) The given data has been used to draw the scatter diagram in Figure 32.1.

Inspection of the scatter diagram gives us some confidence that the points are scattered around an imaginary line and so it is appropriate to try to find this line using the regression equation.

Figure 32.1
Scatter diagram for
Worked Example 32.1

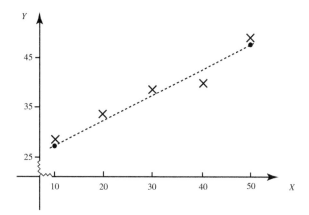

(b) Note from the formulae that we need to add up various quantities, for
example

$$\sum_{i=1}^{n} x_i \quad \sum_{i=1}^{n} x_i y_i$$

In this example, in which there are five individuals, $n = 5$. It is easier to
keep track of the calculations if the intermediate quantities are recorded
in a table of values such as that shown in Table 32.2.

Table 32.2

individual	x_i	y_i	$x_i y_i$	x_i^2
A	10	28	280	100
B	20	32	640	400
C	30	38	1140	900
D	40	39	1560	1600
E	50	48	2400	2500

$$\sum_{i=1}^{5} x_i = 150 \quad \sum_{i=1}^{5} y_i = 185 \quad \sum_{i=1}^{5} x_i y_i = 6020 \quad \sum_{i=1}^{5} x_i^2 = 5500$$

We now have all the quantities we need to calculate b and then a:

$$b = \frac{n \sum_{i=1}^{n} x_i y_i - \left(\sum_{i=1}^{n} x_i\right)\left(\sum_{i=1}^{n} y_i\right)}{n \sum_{i=1}^{n} x_i^2 - \left(\sum_{i=1}^{n} x_i\right)^2}$$

$$= \frac{5(6020) - (150)(185)}{5(5500) - (150)^2}$$

$$= 0.47$$

Then

$$a = \frac{\sum\limits_{i=1}^{n} y_i - b \sum\limits_{i=1}^{n} x_i}{n}$$

$$= \frac{185 - (0.47)(150)}{5}$$

$$= 22.9$$

So the regression equation, $y = a + bx$, is $y = 22.9 + 0.47x$. We can use this equation to predict values of y for any values of x we choose, although it is not advisable to use it to predict values outside the interval of given values of X (that is, 10 to 50).

(c) The easiest way to draw the regression line, $y = 22.9 + 0.47x$, is to find two points which lie on the line. Note that when $x = 10$, $y = 27.6$, so the point (10, 27.6) lies on the line. When $x = 50$, $y = 22.9 + 0.47(50) = 46.4$, so the point (50, 46.4) also lies on the line. The points have been plotted and the line has been drawn in Figure 32.1.

(d) When the value of X is $x = 37$ we find $y = 22.9 + 0.47(37) = 40.29$. You could also use the straight line graph to read off the value of Y corresponding to $X = 37$ although this is not likely to be as accurate as using the equation.

It is relevant to note that computer software packages such as Excel have in-built functions which will calculate regression equations. You should seek advice about the availability of such software within your own institution because with data sets of a realistic size it is pointless trying to perform these calculations by hand.

It is also important to realise that even though we have calculated the regression equation and used it to predict a value of Y, we have no idea how good a prediction this might be. Advanced statistical techniques make it possible to state how confident we can be in our predicted value but these techniques are beyond the scope of this book.

Self-assessment questions 32.2

1. When drawing a scatter diagram for a regression problem, which variable is plotted on the horizontal axis and which on the vertical axis?

2. What is meant by the phrase 'the regression of Y on X'?

3. Explain the meaning of the terms 'predictor' and 'response variable'.

Exercise 32.2

1. Table 32.3 shows values of X and Y measured on six students.

Table 32.3

student	x_i	y_i
A	5	3
B	10	18
C	15	42
D	20	67
E	25	80
F	30	81

   (a) Use a scatter diagram to show that there appears to be a linear relationship between X and Y.
   (b) Find the equation which represents the regression of Y on X.
   (c) Plot the regression line on the scatter diagram.
   (d) Use the equation to predict the value of Y when $X = 12$.

2. It is believed that a certain drug can reduce a patient's pulse rate. In an experiment it was found that the larger the dose of the drug, the more the pulse rate reduced. A doctor wishes to find a regression equation which could be used to predict the pulse rate achieved for specific dosages. An experiment is carried out on four healthy individuals, varying the dose, X (in μg), and measuring the corresponding pulse rate, Y (in beats per minute). The data is shown in Table 32.4.

Table 32.4

individual	dose x_i	pulse rate y_i
A	2	72
B	2.5	71
C	3	65
D	3.5	60

   (a) Use a scatter diagram to show that there appears to be a linear relationship between X and Y.
   (b) Find the equation which represents the regression of Y on X.
   (c) Plot the regression line on the scatter diagram.
   (d) Use the equation to predict the pulse rate expected by administering a dose of 3.2 μg.

Test and assignment exercises 32

1. Calculate the Y on X regression line for the data in Table 32.5. Use the equation to find the value of the response variable when the predictor is 2.5.

Table 32.5

item	x_i	y_i
A	1	2.8
B	2	7.9
C	3	13.4
D	4	18.0

2. Table 32.6 shows values of Statistics Module marks, (X), and Econometrics Module marks, (Y), measured on six students.

Table 32.6

student	x_i	y_i
A	35	22
B	40	38
C	45	52
D	50	68
E	55	65
F	60	73

(a) Use a scatter diagram to show that there appears to be a linear relationship between X and Y.
(b) Find the equation which represents the regression of Y on X.
(c) Plot the regression line on the scatter diagram.
(d) Another student, G, scored 48 in her Statistics Module. What mark in Econometrics would the regression equation predict?